QUICKER QUILTS

QUICKER QUILTS

Linda Rimel

ARCO PUBLISHING, INC.
NEW YORK

Published by Arco Publishing, Inc.
215 Park Avenue South, New York, N.Y. 10003

Library of Congress Cataloging in Publication Data

Rimel, Linda.
  Quicker quilts.

  Includes index.
  1. Quilting. I. Title.
TT835.R54 1984   746.9′7   84-16801
ISBN 0-668-06119-7 (Cloth Edition)
ISBN 0-668-06123-5 (Paper Edition)

Printed in the United States of America

10 9 8 7 6 5 4 3 2 1

Contents

Acknowledgments

The author gratefully acknowledges her debt to:

Mary Rimel, whose contribution of working space and materials made this project possible, and who also suggested the title of "Maple Log Cabin" and the idea for "Reversible Playground Pals";

Ms. Joy A. Daniels, Public Affairs Officer of the Canadian Consulate General in Seattle, and Mr. Graham Glocking of the State Ceremonial Office of the Ministry of the Secretary of State in Ottawa, for their assurances that a quilt incorporating the Canadian flag would not be improper or disrespectful;

Glenn and Kathy Rimel, for the frequent loan of Kathy's camera, and for photographic assistance;

and those who contributed fabric remnants—the late Helen Jane Burgan, Valerie Burgan, Pat Druckenmiller, Melody Heiny, Rhonda Rimel, and Leah Sideras.

Introduction

Traditionally, making a quilt takes months, even years. Some of the quilts in this book can be made in *hours*. *Quicker Quilts* is an attempt to let busy persons quilt.

The book was inspired by the beauty of traditionally made quilts. But these original designs differ significantly from old-fashioned quilts: these are "drudgeless." Unorthodox shortcuts and tools and revolutionarily few pieces go into their streamlined construction. Each quilt is explained independently, like a recipe, so that the reader can make a quilt without first having to read a volume of theory. In addition, each is rated on a scale of relative quickness:

> Q—Quick
> QQ—Quicker
> QQQ—Quicker still
> QQQQ—Quickest

The quilts can be made inexpensively on ordinary sewing machines. Many designs do not even require zigzag attachments. Some *do* call for quilting guides, which sell for as little as $2.00 and come as standard equipment on some machines. Bed sheets—often cheaper per yard than fabric on the bolt—are used whenever possible to keep costs down.

So, sew!

QUICKER QUILTS

Some Basics

Tools for Shortcuts

Some of the tools that make the shortcuts in this book possible are not generally used in sewing:

Large safety pins. Machine quilting is often thought to be impractical because, as Beth Gutcheon writes in *The Perfect Patchwork Primer* (David McKay Company, Inc., 1973, and Penguin Books, Inc., 1974), "The quilt will have to be thread-basted so thoroughly beforehand to prevent the layers from shifting that you might as well quilt by hand." The solution is to "baste" with safety pins—in mere minutes.

The ideal pin size is 1½ inches long, which is smaller than a diaper pin. Unlike the diaper-pin-sized safety pin, the 1½-inch pin has a narrow gauge and will not punch holes in the fabric.

Washable ink markers. They are more accurate and less messy than pencils, chalk, and cornstarch, which are what traditional quilters use. (Please note that although laundering on a warm and gentle cycle is advised throughout the book, you should check the instructions of the manufacturer of your own washable marker to be sure that this is the method recommended for removing the marks made by your pen. For some markers, cold-water washing is recommended. Also, be sure to test the marker on a remnant and assure yourself that the ink will wash out of your fabric, before using the marker on a quilt.)

Weights. Spools, bobbins, cylindrical bearings, small bottles, and even coins can hold large pattern pieces in place on fabric with less fuss than pins.

Most of the tools needed for quicker quilts, however, are conventional sewing equipment. Every quilt does not require all of these tools, but those necessary are listed with the other "ingredients" at the beginning of each quilt "recipe." Among them are:

Fabric shears. Keep them sharpened and cut nothing but fabric with them.

A quilting guide. A simple rod with a blunt hook on one end, the quilting guide allows you to sew parallel lines a uniform distance apart when the guides on the throat plate are covered with the quilt.

An ironing board and an iron. These are absolutely essential to good sewing.

A point turner.

Dritz® Ezy-Hem® Guide by Risdon (designed by Edna Bryte Bishop). Ideal for pressing under edges quickly.

Common pins. Especially good for quilting are pins 1½ inches long with ball points and glass heads.

You will also need some simple drafting tools:

Pattern paper with a 1-inch grid (available at fabric stores).
A straightedge.
A compass.
A French curve.

3

For best results, use a quilting foot for the actual quilt stitching (sewing through the sandwich of quilt top, batting, and quilt bottom). A "quilting foot" may have come as standard equipment on your sewing machine. Or, your machine may have come equipped with a simple, straight-stitch presser foot, sometimes called the "ordinary" (not "zigzag") presser foot; this is also a quilting foot. A quilting foot facilitates smooth, unpuckered quilting.

A Quick Word About Stitch Lengths

Appropriate stitch-length settings are given in both standard and metric measurements for every seam in this book. The standard measurement stitch length is given first, with the metric setting following in parentheses: "a stitch length of 9 (3 for metric machines)." To determine whether to use the standard or the metric number, look at the stitch-length adjustment on your sewing machine. If the settings range from 6 through 20, the machine uses standard measurements, and the numbers correspond to the number of stitches per inch. If the machine has settings of 0 through 4, it uses the metric system, and the settings refer to the number of millimeters per stitch. Because one system calibrates *stitches per unit of measurement* (inch) and the other system calibrates *units of measurements* (millimeters) *per stitch*, the measurements do not convert readily. That is why stitch-length settings in both systems of measurement are provided.

Some machines have stitch-length settings ranging from 1 through 8. They are merely metric settings, doubled. A setting of *8* yields a stitch 4 millimeters long; a setting of *6* yields a stitch length of 3 millimeters; and so on. For this kind of machine, use the metric setting times two.

Stitch-Length setting	6–20	0–4	0–8
System	Standard	Metric	"Double Metric"
Numbers refer to:	Stitches per inch	Millimeters per stitch	Half-millimeters per stitch

Sample stitch-length settings

Ordinary sewing	12	2.5	5
Basting and gathering	6	4	8
Machine quilt stitching	9	3	6
Appliquéing	16	2	4
Satin stitching[1]	20	0.5	1

If you are in doubt about your machine's system of measuring stitch length, you can determine it by (1) consulting the owner's manual; (2) measuring the length, in *millimeters*, of stitches sewn at a given setting (the setting may be an even multiple of the number of millimeters); or (3) counting the number of stitches, sewn at a given setting, *per inch* (on a standard machine a setting of *9* yields 9 stitches per inch, a setting of *12* yields 12 stitches per inch, etc). The range of settings on your machine may be different from 6 through 20—it may be 5 through 15, for example—but the numbers may nonetheless refer to stitches per inch. When you have determined a ratio between your machine's stitch-length settings and the settings listed in one of the columns of the chart above, you may want to make a notation on the chart and refer to it as you sew.

[1]Follow the instructions in the owner's manual, or use a wide zigzag stitch and this setting.

"What if the directions say, "Begin and end the seam by sewing in place with a stitch length of zero," and there is no 'zero' setting on my machine?" Simply:

1. Place the stitch-length-regulating lever exactly in the middle, between forward and reverse settings; *or*
2. Stitch in place by raising the presser foot *very* slightly with one hand while you hold the cloth in place with the other (if this technique is new to you, practice first on a scrap); *or*
3. Use the *embroider* or *darn* setting, or whatever setting drops the feed dogs on your machine.

Quilt Sizes

Sizes are given for each of the designs in this book. If you are designing your own quilt, remember that the size of a quilt depends upon the size of the bed and how much of the bed you want the quilt to cover. Machine quilting is definitely a limiting factor, unless the quilt is quilted in segments which are then pieced together (as in Real Pinwheel, Granddaughter's Flower Garden, Six Moons of Saturn, and Border Print Bedspread), or by adding three layers simultaneously.

These standard mattress sizes provide a starting point:

	Inches
Small crib	22 × 38
Full-size crib	27 × 50
Cot/youth bed	30 × 75
Twin/bunk	39 × 75
Extra-long twin	39 × 80
Double	54 × 75
Extra-long double	54 × 80
Queen	60 × 80
King	78 × 80
California king	72 × 84

A coverlet may be just a few inches larger than the mattress. When planning a bedspread, be sure to measure the distance from the top of the mattress to the floor. Although the standard crib mattress is only 27 inches wide, to allow plenty of margin for tucking around the baby, a crib quilt may be as wide as 48 inches. Baby quilts intended for use on the floor or in buggies may, of course, be any size.

How to Fit Batting

Batting is the cottony insulating fabric between the quilt top and the quilt bottom. Its depth lends texture to the quilt-stitching pattern. Thus, it is important that the batting in the middle of a quilt feel like an uninterrupted piece—even if it is actually several sections pieced together.

When fitting sections of batting to a quilt, use the quilt bottom as a pattern for the proper size.

Do not allow overlapping of batting sections or gaps between them (Figure 1A). Simply lay the sections side by side and lace them together with long hand stitches in white thread (Figure 1B). Neatness doesn't count at this stage. As long as you use white thread, these stitches will never show. When the quilt is finished, the quilt stitching will hold the batting sections together.

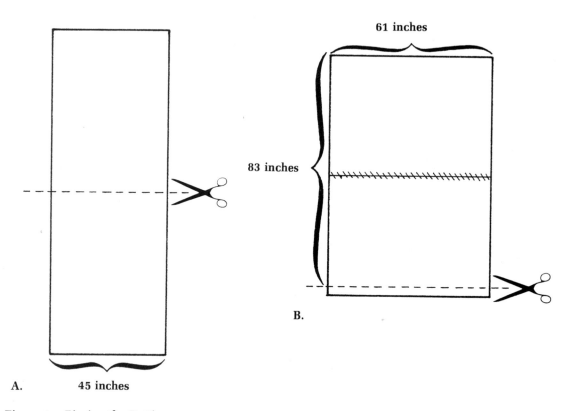

Figure 1.   Piecing the Batting.
A. 45-inch-wide batting is cut into segments to cover a quilt bottom 83 × 61 inches.
B. The batting edges just touch each other without gaps or overlapping. Edges are hand-stitched together with white thread.

Miscellaneous Hints

Batting is extremely porous. It can absorb all the oils from the skin of hands it encounters even briefly, leaving quilters' hands cracked and itching. Spare yourself the agony; use non-greasy hand lotion before and after working with batting. For projects that involve extensive handling of batting, such as the prestuffed unit quilts Granddaughter's Flower Garden, Real Pinwheel, Reversible Cabin Fever and the variation of Maple Log Cabin in which three layers are constructed simultaneously, and Woven Coverlet, wear thin, well-fitted rubber gloves.

For woven coverlets, all hand seams in the batting must run parallel to the stitching lines (the direction of the arrows—see page 111). Otherwise, cutting apart the strands would undo the batting seams.

For prestuffed unit quilts such as Real Pinwheel and Granddaughter's Flower Garden, lace the batting segments together to form a rectangle of the dimensions of the finished quilt. Use the quilt design as a general layout and cutting scheme for the batting. Hold the pattern pieces in place with pattern weights and draw around them with a washable marker. The pieces will not make an exact fit because the seam allowances are included in the pattern pieces. Draw around all the pattern pieces before cutting. Every time you cut across the hand stitches you should immediately tie knots in both ends of the severed thread.

To avoid having stray (and not necessarily white) *threads and lint* permanently encased inside a quilt, *store the batting in a bag* until you are ready to use it. Dust-mop or vacuum the floor *before* you get out the batting.

Bindings

Using quilt binding or blanket binding to encase the raw edges of a quilt is quicker than pressing under the edges and topstitching; the binding also provides a visual "frame" for the work. In a quilt such as Stained Glass Window, binding can even be an integral part of the design. Here are some guidelines:

When two or more lengths of binding must be sewn together, do so *on the bias*. This is not an area for shortcuts; bindings not sewn on the bias come apart on the first trip through the laundry. Open the center fold and pin the ends of the bindings together at right angles to each other, right sides together. Poke a common pin into the fold of the top binding; make sure it exits on the fold of the bottom batting. Use a straightedge and a washable marker to draw a diagonal line (see Figure 2A). With a stitch length of 16 (2 for metric machines), the presser-foot pressure at the tightest setting, and machine set on *silk/satin* or low speed (if your machine has these features), sew over the marked line, taking three to five stitches in place at the beginning and the end. Trim the seam allowances to ¼ inch. Press the seam allowances open. Then fold the binding on the fold line again and press.

Begin pinning the binding onto the quilt's edges. To form a mitered corner, allow the binding to extend beyond the corner of the quilt for a distance equal to the width of the binding (Figure 2B-1). Then form a corner with the binding (Figure 2B-2). Fold the superfluous binding to the inside of the binding, on a diagonal line (2B-3); pin it to the top binding only. Fold the superfluous binding on the bottom in the opposite direction (2B-4); pin.

Instead of mitering corners, you can cut four lengths of binding, press their ends under, and pin them on individually, sides first, ends next (Figure 2C). (This shortcut won't work, however, on woven coverlets, because the binding encases the strand ends and there is no fabric inside the binding at the corners.)

Sew the binding to the quilt by topstitching in parallel rows ½ and ¼ inch away from the inside edge of the binding. If your machine can hold a twin needle, by all means use a twin needle for this (a twin needle is not, however, recommended for the actual quilt stitching of a reversible quilt; the bobbin side is just a zigzag.) Topstitch over the folds at the corners.

Quilt "Extending"

There are, of course, conventional ways to speed the construction of a quilt. Just as a pound of beef can be made to render more servings by extending it with noodles and sour cream than by serving it plain, traditional patchwork quilt blocks can be "extended" by alternating them with simple squares of fabric.

Every other Basket of Scraps block, for example, can be replaced by a plain square for an

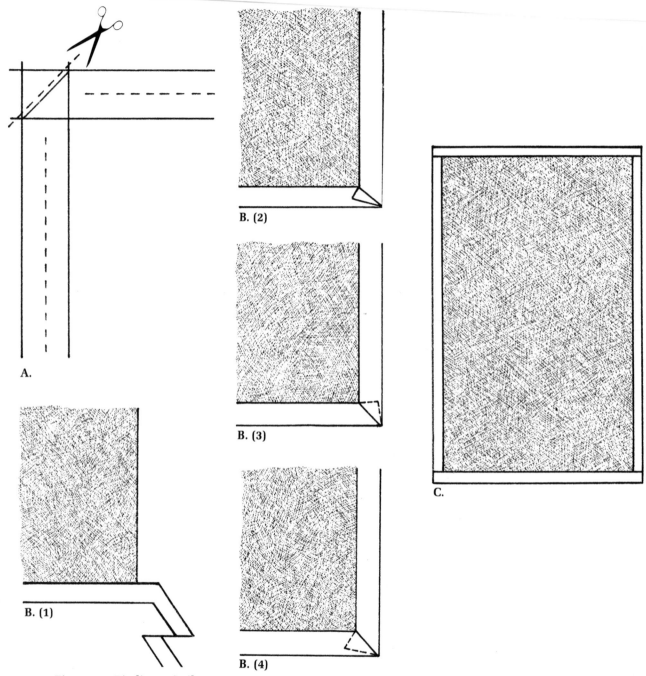

Figure 2. Binding a Quilt.
A. Join two lengths of binding *on the bias* by first opening the center folds (the broken lines) and
    pinning the ends of the bindings together at a right angle, with right sides of the fabric together.
    Mark a diagonal line and sew over it. Trim the seam allowances to ¼ inch.
B. (1) To form a mitered corner, allow the binding to extend beyond the quilt's corner for a distance
       equal to the width of the binding.
    (2) Form a corner with the binding.
    (3) Fold the superfluous binding to the inside of the binding on a diagonal line.
    (4) Fold the superfluous binding in the opposite direction on the bottom.
C. You can apply binding without mitering the corners.

ordinary checkerboard look (Figure 3A). Or, squares made of four Basket of Scraps blocks can alternate with larger plain squares as in Figure 3B.

Kaleido'Scraps combines the efficiency of an "extended" quilt with the visual interplay among the quilt blocks of an unextended quilt (Figure 3C). See also the color photograph of Kaleido'Scraps following page 50, in which the red bandana-print squares are staggered, and a twelve-block diagonal chain is possible. Notice the different layout schemes in the four-block squares.

The *quilting* of "extended" or traditional block quilts can be done by machine *if* the quilt is small enough to be manageable. Prevent the three layers (top, batting, and bottom) from shifting in relation to each other while you quilt by "basting" them together with large safety pins beforehand. Just be sure *not* to sew over the safety pins.

Designing Your Own Quick Quilts

One reason that making quilts from the "recipes" in this book is so quick is that the decision-making process has been eliminated. When you create your own designs, you will have to confront such questions as:

What size will the quilt be?   This is the first question you should ask. Quilts much larger than 65 × 85 inches can't easily be machine-quilted, unless they are (1) constructed in segments, by adding a bedspread's side and end pieces after the center has been quilted (as in Six Moons of Saturn and Border Print Bedspread); (2) constructed by prestuffing units (such as those of Real Pinwheel and Granddaughter's Flower Garden); or (3) constructed by adding three layers—top, batting, and bottom—simultaneously (as in the variations of Maple Log Cabin and Cabin Fever). Obviously, if the quilting is to be done by one of these methods, you need to know that before you begin to cut. Even for a smaller quilt, being able to anticipate the size of the completed work will help you in selecting fabrics and buying batting. Refer to *Quilt Sizes* on page 5.

How much money do you want to spend?   Here are a few factors to consider: (1) A quilt such as Stained Glass Window, which uses yards of binding and trim, or one that uses prequilted fabric, will cost more to make than one that doesn't. (2) Buying batting is more expensive than filling a quilt with a recycled blanket, but the blanket won't show off the quilt-stitching pattern to as great advantage. (3) Usually sheets are cheaper per yard than fabric on the bolt, and it is always cheaper to use scraps you already have than to purchase new fabric. However, a quilt designed around scraps on hand may require you to use many small pieces, making the project time-consuming. At the other extreme, obviously a quilt top or bottom made from one or two sheets cannot have the exciting interplay of colors that a quilt made from many different fabrics can. Expense is an important factor, but one that must be weighed against time and your aesthetic expectations for the quilt.

Do you want to depict a specific image on the quilt?   If so, two words of advice: Stylize. Simplify. Make sure that the image you select will be recognizable if its corners are rounded off and some of its details omitted. For example, photographs of the earth from space are beautiful, but rendering wispy clouds, seas, and half-hidden land masses is too involved for the techniques described in this book. If you are doing a reverse-appliqué quilt, such as Baby's Butterfly, Border Print Quilt, or Maple Log Cabin, remember that the image must be recognizable by its silhouette alone.

Once you have selected an image, draft it to the desired size. First transfer the original image onto graph paper by placing carbon paper between the picture and the graph paper and tracing,

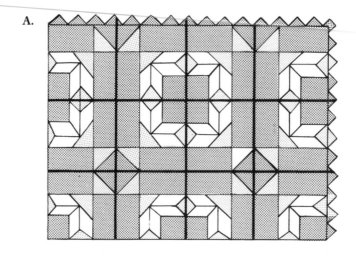

A.

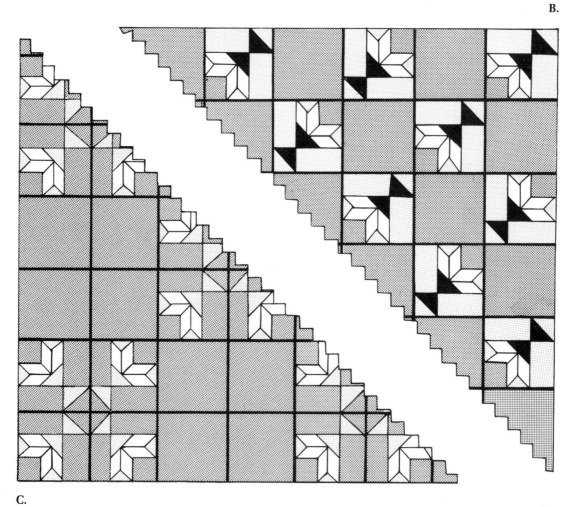

B.

C.

Figure 3.   Stretching Your Traditional Quilt Blocks.
A. A Basket of Scraps quilt.
B. A square of plain fabric replaces every other Basket of Scraps block.
C. Larger plain fabric squares alternate with four-block squares of Basket of Scraps.

or by simply photocopying the image onto a sheet of graph paper. Then decide what scale to use and draft the image onto gridded pattern paper. Be sure to add uniform seam allowances on both sides of every seam.

Is time a major consideration?   Remember that a quilt composed of a few large pieces is less work than one made of many smaller pieces. Moreover, the simpler the image—and the fewer tight corners it has—the easier it will be to incorporate into a quilt. At the quilt-stitching stage, there is obviously less labor involved in sewing parallel rows four inches apart than two inches apart.

When you have the design well in mind, make notes. This will save you from having to rethink the design over and over as you make the quilt. You won't need to write detailed instructions, but jot down the *sequence* of the steps of construction, the size of the seam allowances, and a shopping list of fabric, binding, batting, and notions you will need.

Finally, in general:

Buy bonded batting.
Quilt from the center of the work to the outside edges.
Use a quilting foot.

Care of Quilts

Generally, machine-wash a quilt on a warm and gentle cycle; machine-dry it alternately on warm and fluff (no-heat) settings. Of course, a quilt needs to be treated as delicately as its most delicate component. For best results, launder very large quilts in large commercial machines that have not been used recently for dyeing. If in doubt, precede the quilt with a load of (old) white towels and sheets.

If a quilt comes out of the dryer quite wrinkled, spray the quilt with clean water from a plant mister. The idea is to get the fabric, but not the batting, moistened. Return the quilt to the dryer and dry it on the fluff/no-heat setting. *Never iron a quilt.*

Don't bleach a quilt, unless—as in the case of a baby's quilt—you are prepared to have it depreciate quickly.

Don't line-dry a quilt. The batting will be loft-less where it has hung over the line, and the water will puddle in the ends long after the middle is dry. Moreover, it will take forever to dry.

A trip through the dryer on the no-heat setting will restore the loft to a quilt that has been compressed for gift-wrapping or shipping.

Don't store a quilt in a plastic bag or other airtight container. Even if a quilt seems dry, it may contain enough moisture to mildew. Traditionally, quilts not in use have been stored in the cloth presentation cases in which they come "gift-wrapped."

Another traditional way to store a quilt that is not in use is to hang it on a quilt stand in the bedroom. This method also allows you to show off the quilt.

The Quilts

Cabin Fever (QQQ)

The Cabin Fever quilt is so named because it is a variation of the traditional Log Cabin quilt block (see Figure 4A)—not because anyone will go stir-crazy constructing it. It is easy. Moreover, the instructions accommodate any size bed.

You will need the following:

- fabric for the quilt top (this is a great way to diminish the scrap bag—but reject anything worn or sun-bleached, as well as anything that is not colorfast)
- a new sheet for the quilt bottom
- another sheet or a thin bedspread to serve as a "pattern" (reusable)
- 3.3- to five-ounce *bonded* polyester batting
- thread
- a sewing machine with a size 9 or 11 (European size 65 or 75) needle and a quilting foot
- a Bishop hem guide (Dritz® Ezy-Hem® Guide)
- an ironing board and an iron
- a yardstick
- 60 or so large (1½-inch) safety pins (reusable)
- a washable marker
- common pins
- fabric shears
- a seam ripper

Pick the hems out of the new sheet with the seam ripper. Machine-wash and dry the sheet and the fabric.

Decide what size bedspread or comforter you want. Fold the "reusable" sheet or thin bedspread to these dimensions and lay it on the floor as a pattern.

Assess the fabric. The outer panels of the quilt require more material than the inner ones, so save the large pieces for the outside. You may want to create the impression of a border by making the two outermost panels from a dark color. Select something eye-catching for the center.

Cut the first pair of panels, either on the grain of the fabric or exactly perpendicular to it. *Pairs of panels should be identical.* The two panels should match each other in fabric and width (between 4 and 8 inches). The first pair of panels should be the length of the center panel. Placing right sides of the fabric together, pin the panels to opposite sides of the center panel. Stitch, using a ¼-inch (0.6-cm) seam. Press the seam allowances open.

Position the three-panel unit you've sewn in the center of the sheet "pattern" on the floor. Select another fabric and cut a pair of panels as long as the width of the center piece plus the width of the first pair of panels. (*Hint:* Cut the two new panels by cutting a single extra-long section of fabric, sewing it to one edge of the center pieces, trimming the excess, sewing the excess to the opposite edge of the center pieces, and then trimming off the excess.) Pin and sew the panels onto the ends of the other pieces. Press as before.

Continue adding pairs of panels. Be sure to cut them on the grain of the fabric or perpendicular to it. Vary the width of the panels (but *pairs* must be of equal width) in order to make the quilt

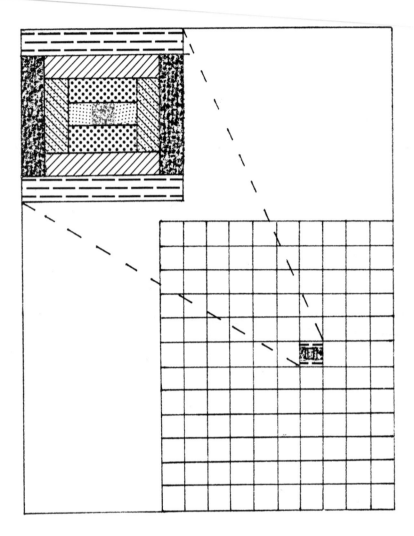

Figure 4.   Cabin Fever.
A. A Cabin Fever quilt is an elongated variation of one block of Log Cabin. A traditional Log Cabin would require dozens of such blocks.

top longer than it is wide. Use the folded sheet as a guide. Add pairs of panels until the quilt top is 2 inches wider and 1½ inches longer than the folded sheet "pattern."

Cut the *new* sheet (for the quilt bottom) the same size as the folded "pattern" sheet. If the sheet is too narrow, fold it in half lengthwise and pin it along the fold. Press in a center crease. Remove the pins. Cut on the crease. To fill the gap, cut a "racing stripe" the length of the sheet from contrasting fabric (Figure 4B). Lay it right side up over the middle of the quilt top. Lay the sheet halves over the quilt top, aligning the sheet's *non-selvage* sides—formerly in the center, the non-selvage sides were created by cutting on the crease—with the sides of the quilt top, and allowing the *selvage* edges to overlap the racing stripe. Pin the sheet halves to the racing stripe.

Figure 4 *continued*   CABIN FEVER (QQQ)   17

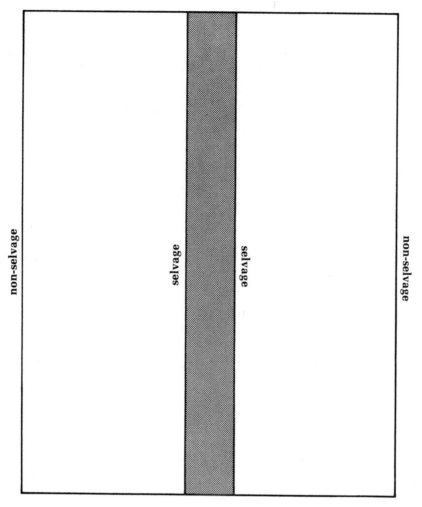

B. If the quilt top is wider than the quilt bottom sheet, fill the gap with a lengthwise strip in a contrasting color.

Topstitch two rows along the sheet halves' selvage edges, ⅛ and ¼ inches from the edges (or, if your machine has this capability, use a twin needle and topstitch one row). Trim the racing stripe's seam allowances to ½ inch and press them toward the outside.

Using the Bishop hem guide, press under ½ inch along the two sides and one end of the quilt top. With right sides together. pin and sew the unpressed quilt top end to an end of the quilt bottom, using a ½-inch (1.2-cm) seam. Press the seam open; fold the wrong sides together on the seam line and press again.

Now lay the quilt top on the floor, wrong side up. Smooth out any wrinkles. Cut the batting to conform to the size of the quilt; it should touch the seam on the sewn end and the folded edges on the other end and the sides. Fold the quilt bottom over the batting and smooth out wrinkles. With five safety pins, pin the quilt bottom to the quilt top along the sewn end to prevent it from "curling." On the unsewn end, fold the folded edge of the quilt top over the edge of the quilt bottom and pin with common pins. Fold and pin the side edges of the quilt top over the side edges of the quilt bottom. *Without picking up the quilt,* secure all three layers together with

Figure 4 continued

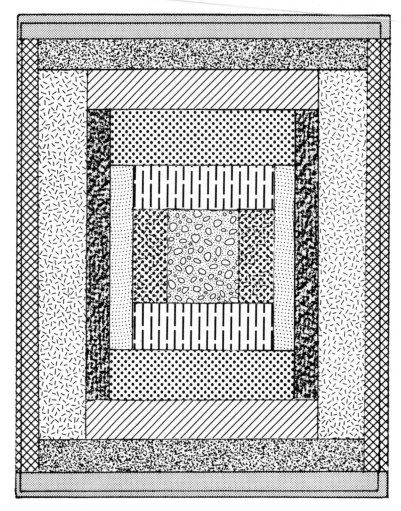

C. A Cabin Fever quilt. Quilt-stitching lines are shown in black.

well-spaced safety pins. Remove the five safety pins along the sewn end and replace them with common pins perpendicular to the edge.

Fill a bobbin with thread matching the quilt bottom sheet. There will probably be so many colors in the quilt top that any neutral color will do for top thread. With a stitch length of 12 (2.5 for metric machines), topstitch ⅛ and ¼ inch from the seam along the sewn end, and the same distances from the folds on the borders of the quilt bottom.

To do the machine quilting, simply topstitch over the seam lines (Figure 4C), starting in the center and working outward. (Traditionally, this is called quilting in the ditch.) Set the stitch length at 9 (3 for metric machines). Release the presser-foot pressure slightly. To begin, position the needle over one end of a seam between the center piece and a panel. With one hand above the quilt and the other below it, smooth out wrinkles along the quilting line. Lower the needle and the presser foot. With the stitch-length regulator at zero, take three to five stitches in place. Then follow the seam to the corner, removing pins in your path. *Don't stitch over safety pins.* Stop periodically to place hands above and below the quilt and smooth out wrinkles. At the corner leave the needle in the fabric, raise the presser foot, and turn the quilt 90 degrees. With both hands, smooth out the fabric along the seam line. Lower the presser foot and stitch over the seam. To "tie off" the quilt stitching at the end of a seam, take three to five stitches in place, cut the bobbin thread and clip the top thread close to the quilt top. Quilt-stitch over all the seam lines. Then quilt-stitch 1 inch away from the outside edge around the perimeter, and quilt-stitch a ¾-inch cross in the center of the center panel.

Clip the ends of the threads on the reverse side.

That's it. Your sight and sanity are still intact. The quilt you've just made is durable and fully washable (warm cycle); dry it alternately on permanent press and fluff cycles. Don't line-dry or press it.

Variation: Reversible Cabin Fever (Q)

A very large Cabin Fever would be difficult to quilt by machine. This variation eliminates the need for quilting. It also allows you to make a reversible quilt with different colors top and bottom. The three layers are constructed simultaneously.

The dimensions of each bottom piece will, however, have to equal those of the corresponding top piece. Begin by cutting the center rectangle for the quilt top, a rectangle the same size for the quilt bottom, and a piece of batting the same size as well. Lay the batting over the *wrong* side of the bottom piece, and lay the top piece over the batting, *right side up*; pin around all four edges with common pins. With the presser-foot pressure slightly loosened, use a size 14 (European size 90) needle and a stitch length of 6 (4 for metric machines) to baste around the perimeter, ¼ inch (0.6 cm) from the edge.

Cut the first pair of panels for the quilt top. Remember: pairs of panels must be of identical fabric and width (width should range from 4 to 8 inches). Cut the fabric for the first pair of panels to the desired *width*, and pin it to one edge of the center rectangle. Trim the fabric to the proper length. Unpin this panel and use it as a pattern to cut its pair, the first pair of panels for the quilt bottom, and two pieces of batting.

Pin the panels of the quilt bottom to opposite edges of its center rectangle, right sides together. Lay the batting over the bottom panels, remove the pins one at a time, and replace them through all the layers. Turn the quilt over. On the quilt top, lay the quilt top's panels over the pinned edges of the center rectangle, right sides together, and pin. Turn the quilt over and remove all the pins with heads on the quilt bottom.

Sew, using a size 14 (European size 90) needle, a quilting foot, a stitch length of 12 (2.5 for metric machines), and a ¼-inch (0.6-cm) seam. *Be sure that the batting is facing downward.* Leave the presser-foot pressure slightly loosened. You won't need to press the seams or trim the seam allowances (however, if the batting's seam allowances exceed the fabric's ¼-inch (0.6-cm) seam allowances, trim the batting even with the other seam allowances). Before proceeding to the next step, make sure that all three layers have been caught in the seam.

Cut fabric for the next pair of panels to the desired width. Before pinning each strip to the edge of the center rectangle and the ends of the first pair of panels, pin the ends of the first pair of panels through top, bottom, and batting layers to keep the ends square. Cut the new panel fabric to the proper length. Then cut out the other top panel, the batting, and the second pair of quilt-bottom panels, using the first panel as a pattern.

Pin the bottom panels to the opposite edges of the center rectangle and the ends of the first pair of sewn panels, with right sides together. Lay the batting over the bottom panels, remove the pins one at a time, and replace them through all the layers. Turn the quilt over. On the quilt top lay the quilt top's panels over the pinned edges of the center rectangle plus the ends of the first pair of sewn panels, with right sides together; pin. Turn the quilt bottom over and remove all pins with heads on the quilt bottom.

Sew, with the batting facing downward against the throat plate of the sewing machine. Trim the batting's seam allowance if it seems excessive. Before proceeding to the next step, make sure that all layers have been caught in the seam.

Continue adding pairs of panels until the quilt is as big as you want it (Figure 5). All seams are ¼-inch (0.6-cm). *Remember to check each seam before adding the next pair of panels.* The panels may range from 4 to 8 inches in width, but *pairs* of quilt top panels *must* be identical to each other in size and fabric, and the quilt bottom's panels *must* match each other in fabric and be the same dimensions as their counterparts on the quilt top.

There is no quilt stitching.

Finish the quilt's edges by encasing them in quilt binding or blanket binding.

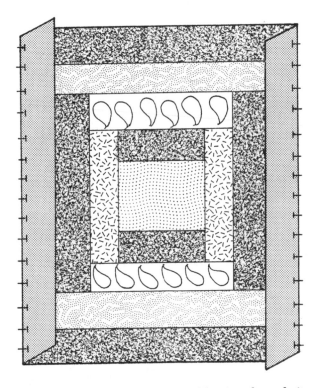

Figure 5.   A Cabin Fever that does not need quilting. Add pairs of panels (top, bottom, and batting) until the quilt is as big as you want it. One line of stitching serves as both seam and quilting. Sew with the batting facing downward against the throat plate.

Baby Dragons (QQ)

While a traditional quilt block may require more than forty pieces, a block of Baby Dragons uses only two—and only *one* pattern piece. The construction is so streamlined that assembling this baby quilt is a bit like learning a card trick. Outlining the quilt-top design with machine quilt stitching transforms the simple geometry of the quilt bottom; dragons and diamonds "magically" appear—without the fuss of a stencil.

To make it you will need:

- 1⅞ square yards of a print or a solid color cotton (Color A)
- 1⅞ square yards of another (Color B)
- an old washable blanket, at least 50 × 40 inches, or 3.3-ounce *bonded* polyester batting the same size
- thread
- a sewing machine with a size 9 or 11 (European size 65 or 75) needle, a zigzag attachment, and a quilting foot
- a Bishop hem guide (Dritz® Ezy-Hem® Guide)
- an ironing board and an iron
- cardboard with a square corner
- a yardstick
- a washable marker
- 30 large (1½-inch) safety pins (reusable)
- common pins
- paper-cutting scissors
- fabric shears

Prewash (by machine) and dry the fabric and the old blanket.

Cut the pieces for the quilt bottom: four 25½ × 20½-inch rectangles, two of Color **A**, two of Color **B**, and two 5-inch squares of each color. Set these pieces aside.

Make the triangular pattern piece. Starting at one corner of the cardboard, measure 5½ inches away from the corner along both adjoining edges; mark. With a straightedge and a pencil, connect the marks. Cut on the line.

On the wrong side of the fabric, draw around the cardboard pattern with a washable marker, as shown in Figure 6A. For fabric with a stripe, use the alternative layout shown. Cut 80 triangles of Color **A** and 80 of Color **B**.

Pin each Color **A** triangle to a Color **B** triangle along the hypotenuse (the long edge), with right sides of the fabric together. Pin carefully—because they are cut on the bias, the fabrics will tend to stretch. Stitch. *All seams are to be ¼-inch (0.6-cm) wide with a stitch length of 12 (2.5 for metric machines).* Begin the seam by taking three to five stitches in place with the stitch-length regulator temporarily set at zero. At the seam's end take three to five stitches in place. *Do not cut the thread.* Leaving only an inch of slack thread between pieces, sew together the next pair of pinned triangles. You will have a quilt-block chain.

When all the seams are sewn, drape the chain of pieces over the ironing board (Figure 6B). To press the seams open, cut the end piece off the chain by snipping the thread; place it wrong side up on the ironing board. Press the Color **A** side from the unsewn corner to—but not *over*—the

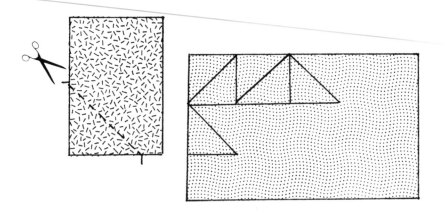

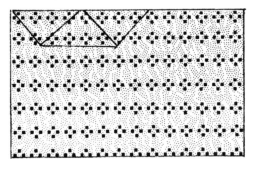

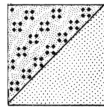

A.

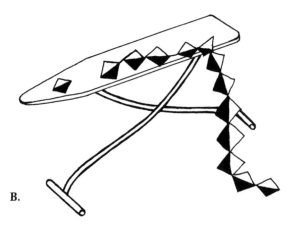

B.

Figure 6. Baby Dragons.
A. (Upper left) Cut a stiff pattern piece from cardboard. With a washable marker, draw around the
   cardboard on the fabric (upper right). For striped fabric, use the layout in the lower left. Lower
   right: every quilt block consists simply of a triangle of Color A sewn to a triangle of Color B.
B. Sew each Color A triangle to a Color B triangle. Do not cut the slack thread between seams. Drape
   the chain of pieces over the ironing board; cut off the end piece, press its seam open, and stack the
   pieces in order.

Figure 6 continued

C. The numbering system for the quilt blocks.

seam, and the Color **B** side to the seam. Part the bottom edge of the seam allowances with your index finger. Run the finger halfway up the seam line, opening the seam allowances. Start pressing at the bottom edge of the open seam allowances; follow your finger to the top. Press all seams open.

Lay out the squares (the quilt blocks), using Figure 6C as a guide. Double-check the layout. Sew vertical seams: with right sides together, pin the right-hand edge of Block **A1** to the left-hand edge of Block **A2**. Place the pinned blocks in a stack. Pin Block **A3** to **A4**; place them on top of the stack. Pin **A5** to **A6**, and **A7** to **A8**; place them in order on the stack. Repeat for rows **B** through **J**.

Starting with the top pair of pinned blocks, sew. Stitch in place at the beginning and the end of every seam. *Do not cut threads between seams.* When all seams are sewn, drape the chain of sewn pieces over the ironing board. Starting with the last piece sewn, cut off the pieces one at a time, press the seams open, and lay the pieces in a stack. Cut, press, and stack each piece, one at a time.

Lay out the pieces again, starting with **J8**, which is on the top of the stack. Double-check the

Figure 6 continued

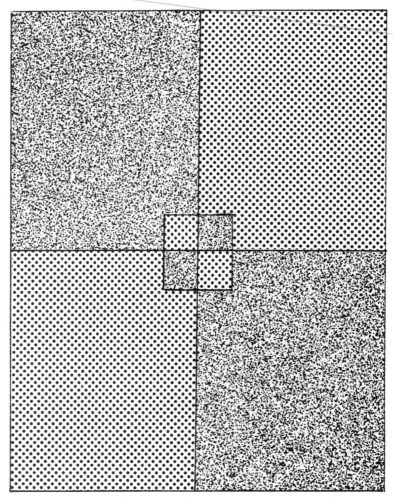

D. The quilt bottom. Squares in the center are machine-appliquéd over the large rectangles.

layout. Pin vertical seams: **A2** to **A3**, **A6** to **A7**, **B2** to **B3**, **B6** to **B7**, etc. Stack as before. Stitch, press, and stack.

Lay out the pieces again, starting with **J8**, which is on the top. Double-check the layout. Pin the remaining vertical seams: **A4** to **A5**, **B4** to **B5**, etc. Stack, stitch, press, and stack.

Lay out the pieces again, starting with Row **J**, which is on the top of the stack. Double-check the layout. Pin the horizontal seams, with right sides together, and matching vertical seams. Pin Row **A** to Row **B**, **C** to **D**, **E** to **F**, **G** to **H**, and **I** to **J**. Stack, stitch, press, and stack.

Lay out the pieces. Double-check. Pin horizontal seams **B** to **C** and **H** to **I**. Sew, press, and lay out again. Double-check. Pin **D** to **E**; sew and press. Pin **F** to **G**; sew and press.

To make the quilt bottom (Figure 6D), lay out the large rectangles as shown in the illustration. Pin and sew the upper left rectangle to the upper right, and the lower left rectangle to the lower right, with right sides together. Press the seams open. Then pin and sew the upper half to the lower half with right sides together; press.

Lay out the squares as illustrated. Sew lefts to rights and press. Sew uppers to lowers and

Figure 6 continued

E. Broken lines indicate machine-quilting lines.

press. Using the Bishop hem guide, press under the outside edges of the squares ¼ inch. Lay the four squares over the four rectangles, aligning the centers and the seams; pin. Machine-appliqué the squares onto the rectangles by sewing with a narrow zigzag stitch and a stitch length setting of 12 (2.5 for metric machines) over the outside edges of the squares. You will be stitching along the fold line where you turned the raw edges under.

Press under ¼ inch along one end and both sides of the quilt top and the quilt bottom. With right sides together, pin and stitch the unpressed end of the quilt top to the unpressed end of the quilt bottom. Press the seam open; fold along the seam lines with wrong sides together and press again.

Lay the quilt bottom on a flat surface, wrong side up. Smooth out any wrinkles. Trim the old blanket (or the batting) to the proper size; it should touch the seam on the sewn end and touch the fold lines on the other edges. Fold the quilt top over the blanket (or batting). Smooth out wrinkles. Pin the edges of the quilt top and the quilt bottom together with common pins. *Without lifting the quilt*, secure all three layers of the quilt together with well-spaced safety pins.

Poke common pins through the quilt top at the very center and at several points along the center vertical and the center horizontal seams; if the pins emerge off-center on the quilt bottom, remove the safety pins, adjust, and repin.

To machine-quilt, simply topstitch over the quilting lines indicated in Figure 6E. Set the stitch length at 9 (3 for metric machines) and release slightly the pressure on the presser foot. Begin by placing a hand above and a hand below the quilt to smooth out wrinkles. Take three to five stitches in place with the stitch length regulator temporarily set on zero. Sew along the quilting lines, stopping periodically to smooth out wrinkles with both hands and to remove pins in your path. *Don't stitch over safety pins.* At corners leave the needle in the fabric, raise the presser foot and turn the quilt. Placing a hand above and a hand below, smooth out wrinkles. Lower the presser foot and sew. At seam's end take three to five stitches in place. When the quilt stitching is finished, clip threads and remove any remaining pins.

Finish by topstitching, with a stitch length of 16 (2 for metric machines) around the perimeter of the quilt, ⅛ and ¼ inch from the edge.

Now all you have to do is to wrap the quilt for the baby shower! You might tell the parents that the quilt is machine-washable and can be tumble-dried on warm settings, but that it shouldn't be pressed or line-dried.

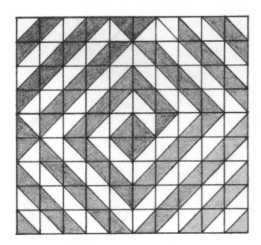
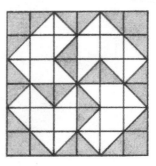

Figure 7.   **Squares made from two triangles can be arranged in many different, striking patterns.**

Variations Using the Same Quilt Block (QQ)

The quilt block used in Baby Dragons—a square made of two right triangles—is one of the most versatile components of patchwork. You can apply the streamlined assembly method of Baby Dragons to variations of that design that (1) use larger (or smaller) blocks; (2) require more (or fewer) blocks; (3) arrange the blocks in patterns other than that of Baby Dragons; and (4) incorporate blocks of whole squares of fabric into the design. See Figure 7.

To make a larger or smaller pattern piece, first decide on the size block you want. Then add ½ inch (representing two ¼-inch seam allowances) to that number. For example, for 8-inch blocks, adding ½ inch to 8 inches yields 8½ inches. Construct an 8½-inch square on pattern paper; bisect it diagonally, forming two triangles. Use one of the triangles as a pattern piece. For best results, lay the pattern paper triangle over a corner of a cardboard with a square corner—say, from a tablet back—and cut the cardboard the same size. Use the cardboard pattern when you cut fabric—and use ¼-inch seams when you sew.

Some alternative layouts are shown, but you will probably enjoy creating your own. Graph paper is good to experiment with.

Stained Glass Window (QQQ)

The look of Victorian elegance is achieved by machine-appliquéing—zigzag stitching—shapes onto the background fabric of this double-bed coverlet. The machine quilt stitching is done without a stencil. See the color photograph following page 50.

To make it you will need:

- a new solid-color flat twin sheet for the quilt top
- another new flat twin sheet, either solid or print, for the quilt bottom
- ⅓ yard of 44-inch or wider fabric for the border diamonds
- fabric for four 12-inch squares
- ¼ yard fabric at least 40 inches wide for the inner "diamond"
- 1 square yard of fabric for the inner square
- 18 yards of wide bias tape in a dark color
- 8¾ yards of quilt binding in the same dark color
- 4 square yards of 4-ounce *bonded* polyester batting
- thread in the same dark color
- thread to match the quilt-top sheet
- thread to match the quilt-bottom sheet
- a sewing machine with a size 9 or 11 (European size 65 or 75) needle, a zigzag attachment, and a quilting foot
- a Bishop hem guide (Dritz® Ezy-Hem® Guide)
- an ironing board and an iron
- a yardstick
- pattern paper with a 1-inch grid
- a washable marker
- common pins
- 60 or so large (1½-inch) safety pins (reusable)
- fabric shears
- a seam ripper

Remove one hem from each sheet, using the seam ripper. Machine-wash and dry the sheets and the fabric.

Cut the top sheet to 61½ × 83½ inches. Align one of its corners with a corner of the bottom sheet. Safety-pin the sheets together on all edges. Using the top sheet as a guide, cut the second sheet to match it. Unpin.

Fold the top sheet in half lengthwise and pin. Press in a center crease. Remove the pins. Fold the sheet in half widthwise; pin and press in a crease. Remove the pins.

Cut out the four 12-inch border squares. Press under ½ inch on two adjoining edges of each square. Position the squares on the sheet's corners with the raw edges of the square facing outward; pin. Machine-baste the squares in place with topstitching ¼ inch (0.6 cm) from the edge along all four sides, using a stitch length of 6 (4 for metric machines).

With the washable marker, mark the borders: merely draw straight lines connecting the innermost corner of one square with the innermost corner of the next square (see Figure 8A). To locate the center border line, fold the outside edge to the marked border line; pin and press in a

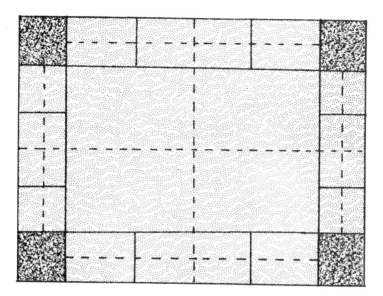

Figure 8. Stained Glass Window.
A. Crease along the dash lines. With a washable marker mark the solid lines.

crease. *Don't press over the marked lines*; steam will cause the washable ink lines to run.

To mark the position of the border diamonds on each quilt *end* (the shorter two edges), measure and mark points 8¼ inches to the left and right of the border's center along the outside edge and the marked border line. With a straightedge and a marker, connect the points. On each *side* border, mark points 13¾ inches either side of the center crease along the outside edge and the marked border line. Connect the points.

Cut and set aside two lengths of bias tape 61½ inches long and two lengths 83½ inches long. Then center bias tape segments over the lines inside the borders (see Figure 8B); pin them in place. With a medium zigzag stitch, a stitch length of 16 (2 for metric machines), top thread matching the bias tape, and bobbin thread matching the bottom sheet, machine-appliqué over the edge of the bias tapes. The stitching should be half on/half off the edge of the bias tapes. Pin and machine-appliqué the bias tapes over the center border lines.

Draw a pattern for the border diamonds: draw a line 11½ inches long. Through its center draw a perpendicular line 6 inches long. With a straightedge connect the ends of the lines. Using this pattern, cut eight border diamonds. Press under ¼ inch around the edges. Position the diamonds over the bias tapes, aligning the corners of the diamonds over the center of the tapes. Pin. Appliqué the diamonds.

Make patterns for the large "diamond" and the square: draw a vertical line 39 inches long. Through its center draw a perpendicular line 28 inches long (14 inches on each side of the 39-inch line). Connect the ends of the lines. Mark points 14 inches above and below the center of the 39-inch line; connect these points to the ends of the perpendicular line. Cut out the 28-inch square you've just made; using it for a pattern, cut fabric for the center square. Cut out one of the triangles bordering the square on the pattern paper. Cut a ¼-inch-wide strip of pattern paper and tape it to each of the three edges of the triangle, to allow for seams. Cut four of these triangles from fabric, *two with the pattern piece upside down.*

With right sides together, pin the short edge of one triangle to the short edge of another; stitch, using a ¼-inch (0.6-cm) seam and a stitch length of 16 (2 for metric machines); press the seam open. Sew the other pair of triangles together and press. With right sides together, pin the

Figure 8 continued

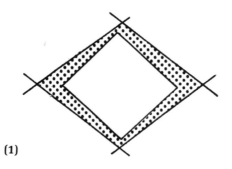

(1)

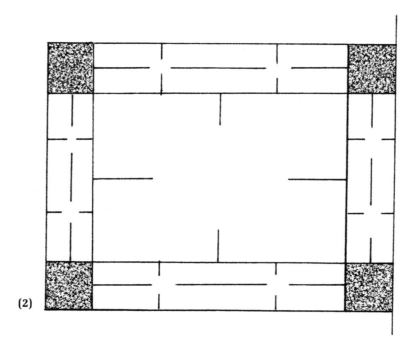

(2)

B. (1) Above: Sew bias tapes to the outside of the center piece.
(2) Below: Center the bias tapes over the lines shown in black.

inside edges of the triangles to the square; stitch and press. Sew the other pair of triangles to the square and press.

Cut four lengths of bias tape 2 inches longer than the sides of the large diamond. With right sides together, pin the tapes to the edges of the diamond, leaving 1 inch of extra tape at each end.

Stitch with a ¼-inch (0.6-cm) seam and a stitch length of 12 (2.5 for metric machines); press.

Position the center piece over the center creases. Cut four lengths of bias tape that are 1 inch longer than the distance from the "diamond"'s corners to the marked border lines. Press under one end of each bias tape ¼ inch and position it over the raw edges of the bias tapes sewn onto the "diamond." The fold should touch the corner of the diamond (the fabric). Pin the center piece and the bias tapes in place, and machine-appliqué over inside, outside, and end edges of the tapes.

Center the 61½-inch strips over the marked border lines of the ends and the edges of the corner squares; pin and machine-appliqué. Center the 83½-inch tapes over the side border lines and the edges of the corner squares; pin and machine-appliqué.

Lay the bottom sheet on the floor, wrong side up. Smooth out any wrinkles. Cut the batting the same size and lay the batting over the quilt bottom. Lay the quilt top, right side up, over the batting. Smooth out the wrinkles. *Without lifting the quilt,* secure its three layers together with well-distributed safety pins. Pin on the quilt binding, encasing ½ inch of the quilt's raw edges inside it, and mitering the corners (see page 7). Machine straight-stitch with a stitch-length setting of 12 (2.5 for metric machines) twice, ⅛ and ¼ inch (or once, with a twin needle) around the perimeter to secure the quilt binding to the quilt.

Quilt Stained Glass Window by machine. With bobbin thread matching the bottom sheet and top thread matching the top sheet, simply straight-stitch on the lines shown in the illustrations (⅛ inch outside the bias tapes). Begin a row of quilt stitching by releasing the pressure on the presser foot slightly and setting the stitch-length adjustment for 9 (3 for metric machines). Placing one hand above and one hand below the quilt along the quilting line, smooth out wrinkles. Lower the needle into the work. Lower the presser foot. With the stitch length temporarily set on zero, take three to five stitches in place. Then sew to the end of the quilting line. At corners leave the needle inserted in the quilt, raise the presser foot, pivot the quilt, smooth out wrinkles with hands above and below the quilt, lower the presser foot, and continue. *Don't sew over safety pins;* remove them as you come to them. At the end of a quilting line, take three to five stitches in place, cut the bobbin thread, and clip the thread close to the quilt. Proceed carefully, and periodically use both hands to check for wrinkles.

Clip the bobbin threads. Launder the quilt on warm and gentle settings. Machine-dry alternately on permanent press and fluff cycles. *Do not press or line-dry.*

Hot Air Balloon (Q)

Dreaming is breezy under this double-bed-size bedspread (ideal size: 84 inches square, to tuck inside a *king-size* waterbed frame). Creating the three-dimensional look is easy; all the quilt stitching is done (by machine, of course) *before* the stuffed balloon is added.

To be up, up, and away, you will need:

- a new blue flat twin sheet
- another new flat twin sheet
- fabric for seven balloon sections, seven balloon section facings, the balloon neck, the balloon mouth, the stripes, the gondola, and the border squares and rectangles: raid your scrap bag!
- 6 inches of trim for the gondola "handle"
- 5½ square yards of 3.3-ounce *bonded* polyester batting
- additional batting or washable pillow fill to stuff the balloon
- thread—blue to match the sheet, black, and white
- a sewing machine with a zigzag attachment, a quilting guide, a size 9 or 11 (European size 65 or 75) needle, and a quilting foot
- a Bishop hem guide (Dritz® Ezy-Hem® Guide)
- an ironing board and an iron
- a yardstick
- a French curve
- a pencil
- pattern paper with a 1-inch grid
- a washable marker
- common pins
- 80 or so large (1½-inch) safety pins (reusable)
- paper-cutting scissors
- fabric shears
- a seam ripper

Remove one hem from each sheet, using the seam ripper. Prewash and dry the fabrics and sheets by machine.

On pattern paper, draft the pattern pieces. Draw a 12-inch square and a 12 × 6¼-inch rectangle. Using Figure 9A as a guide, draw the patterns for the gondola, the stripes, the balloon sections, the balloon neck, and the balloon mouth. Enlarge each square in the illustration to 1 square inch on your grid. Perforate the stripe-placement lines on the balloon sections by sewing over them without thread with a stitch length of 9 (3 for metric machines).

Using the balloon-section pattern piece, cut seven balloon sections and seven facings. Mentally number the balloon sections, starting at the left. With the stripe patterns right side up, cut four upper stripes and four lower stripes. Invert the pattern pieces and cut three upper and three lower stripes. Press under ¼ inch of the two long edges of the stripes. With the washable marker draw the stripe lines on balloon Sections 2 through 6, by placing the pattern over the section and scrubbing gently over the perforated lines with the marker. The stripes should slant upward in Sections 3 and 5, and downward in Sections 2, 4, and 6. (Invert the balloon section pattern piece to mark the downward-slanting stripes.) Pin the stripes onto Sections 2 through 6.

Topstitch them in place ⅛ inch from each edge with a stitch length of 16 (2.5 for metric machines). Lay Section 2 over the right half of Section 1; lay Section 6 over the left half of Section 7. Position the stripes on Section 1 so that they align *at the center* of Section 1 with *the outside edge* of Section 2. Position the stripes on Section 7 so that they align *at the center* of Section 7 with *the outside edge* of Section 6. Pin and topstitch the stripes in place.

Pin each balloon section to a facing, right sides together. Sew a ½-inch (1.2-cm) seam around the perimeter. Do not leave an opening. Clip the curves and trim the seam allowances. Cut a horizontal slash in the *facing* to within ½ inch of the seam on each side. (Be sure not to clip into the seam stitching.) Turn the balloon section right side out through the slash. Press the section flat.

With long hand-stitches, baste Sections 2 through 6 together at the sides, to 1½ inches from the top. The sections should just touch each other *without* overlapping. The outer balloon Sections—1 and 7—are to be narrower than the others: overlap Sections 2 and 6 halfway over Sections 1 and 7, respectively. Baste. With black thread, a wide zigzag setting, and a stitch length of 20 (0.5 for metric machines), sew over the basting. Stuff the balloon sections through the horizontal slashes in the facings. Cut more horizontal slashes as needed. Stuff only the outside halves of Sections 1 and 7. With long hand-stitches, close the slashes in the facings.

Cut 20 12-inch squares and 12 12 × 6¼-inch rectangles for the borders. Sew the border pieces together with ¼-inch (0.6-cm) seams. Press the seam allowances open. Lay the border right side up on the floor. With right sides together, pin a selvage edge (the long, tightly woven edges are the selvage edges) of the blue sheet to an inside edge of the border, leaving a 1-inch margin for error at the starting end of the sheet. Sew a ¼-inch (0.6-cm) seam and press it. Lay the border and the sheet right side up on the floor, spreading the sheet flat and laying the three unsewn border edges over the sheet. On the end of the sheet next to the 1-inch margin, fold the border back over the sheet (with right sides together). Pin and stitch; press.

Lay the sheet and the border right sides up on the floor, again with the unsewn border edges over the sheet. Turn the border back over the sheet along the unsewn selvage; pin, sew, and press. Lay the sheet and the border right side up on the floor again and lay the remaining unsewn border edge back over the sheet. Pin. Trim away the excess sheet and save the remnant. Sew and press.

Cut out the gondola, the balloon neck, and the balloon mouth, and press under ¼ inch along the edges. Position these pieces and the stuffed balloon on the blue background sheet. (Hint: Placing the balloon slightly off-center and the gondola at an angle will suggest motion.) Pin the neck and the gondola in place. The upper edge of the neck goes beneath the balloon. With a washable marker, draw around the outside of the balloon. "Machine-appliqué"—that is, sew with a wide zigzag setting, a stitch length of 20 (0.5 for metric machines), and blue thread over the edges of the balloon neck and the *sides and bottom only* of the gondola. Pin the balloon mouth over the neck and machine-appliqué it in place.

Position the trim "handle" over the gondola, tucking the ends under the top edges of the gondola. With a straightedge and a washable marker, draw the ropes. Three ropes should extend from the center of the "handle" to the upper edge of the mouth; four should extend from the center of the "handle" to the lower edge of the mouth. Remove the trim "handle." With black thread, a narrow zigzag setting, and a stitch length of 20 (0.5 for metric machines), sew the ropes. Pin the "handle" in place and machine topstitch (for thick trim, hand-stitch) it with white thread. Machine-appliqué over the upper edge of the gondola.

Draw straight quilting lines from the lower corners of the balloon neck to the upper corners of the gondola. Use a yardstick or straightedge and a washable marker.

Fold the second sheet in half lengthwise; pin it on the fold and press in a crease. Remove the pins and cut on the crease. Lay the quilt top right side up on the floor. Lay the sheet halves over opposite sides of the quilt top, with the sheet's selvage edges toward the center. Piece together the remnants of the blue sheet to fill the gap between the sheet halves. Lay the selvage edges of the second sheet over the blue center section; pin. Topstitch ⅛ and ¼ inch (or use a twin needle if you can) from the selvage edge of the second sheet, using a stitch length of 12 (2.5 for metric machines). With right sides together, pin one side of the quilt top to a side of the quilt bottom, leaving a 1-inch margin for error. Sew a ½-inch (1.2-cm) seam. Press the seam allowances open; then fold wrong sides together and press again. Lay the quilt bottom wrong side up on the floor and fold the quilt top over it. Trim away the excess length and width (if any) of the quilt bottom. Press under ½ inch of the remaining quilt top and bottom edges.

Lay the quilt bottom on the floor, wrong side up. Smooth out any wrinkles. Cut and piece the batting to the appropriate size; it should touch the seam on the sewn edge and the fold on the pressed edges. Fold the quilt top over the batting. With common pins pin the outside edges of the quilt top to the quilt bottom, beginning on the sewn edge. *Without lifting the quilt,* secure all three layers together with well-spaced safety pins. Release the pressure on the presser foot slightly and topstitch ⅛ and ¼ inch from the outside, or use a twin needle and topstitch once.

Quilt-stitch, using blue thread and a straight stitch. Leave the pressure on the presser foot slightly released. Set the stitch length for 9 (3 for metric machines). The first row of stitching runs around the gondola, along the marked gondola-to-mouth lines, around the outside of the balloon neck, and ¼ inch *inside* the balloon's outline. *Do not stitch over safety pins.* Begin by setting the stitch length at zero and taking three to five stitches in place. Proceed carefully: place a hand above and a hand below the quilt to smooth out wrinkles along the quilting line. Stitch along the quilting line, removing pins as you come to them. At corners, leave the needle in the fabric, but raise the presser foot; turn the quilt, lower the presser foot, and continue. "Tie off" the thread at the end by taking three to five stitches in place.

Remove the quilt from the machine. With a washable marker and a straightedge, draw a parallel line 3 inches distant from the first quilting line around the gondola. Mark the pivot lines above the balloon as shown in the illustration: from every junction of two balloon sections, draw a straight line outward.

Set the quilting guide attachment for 3 inches. Stitch the second row of quilt stitching 3 inches outside, and parallel to, the first row. At the pivot lines, leave the needle in the fabric, raise the presser foot, and turn the quilt so that the quilt guide aligns itself with the arc of the next balloon section in the first stitching line. Lower the presser foot and stitch to the next pivot line. Stitch over the marked lines around the gondola. Stitch the third and subsequent concentric rings of the quilt stitching, pivoting on the pivot lines. Stop at the edge of the blue background. Mark the starting points for the new quilting rows if necessary (see Figure 9B).

Quilt-stitch over the seam lines between the border pieces. After marking them with a washable marker and a straightedge, quilt-stitch the T's on the corner squares, as shown in the illustration.

Safety-pin-baste the balloon in place. Then release most of the pressure on the presser foot. With blue thread, a wide zigzag stitch, and a stitch length of 20 (0.5 for metric machines), machine-appliqué the balloon in place. Remove pins as you come to them.

Clip the thread ends. Remove any visible basting threads. Wash on a warm and gentle cycle to remove ink lines (or follow the manufacturer's instructions for removing marker lines). Tumble-dry alternately on permanent press and fluff cycles. For best results, use a large, commercial dryer.

Sweet dreams and soft landings!

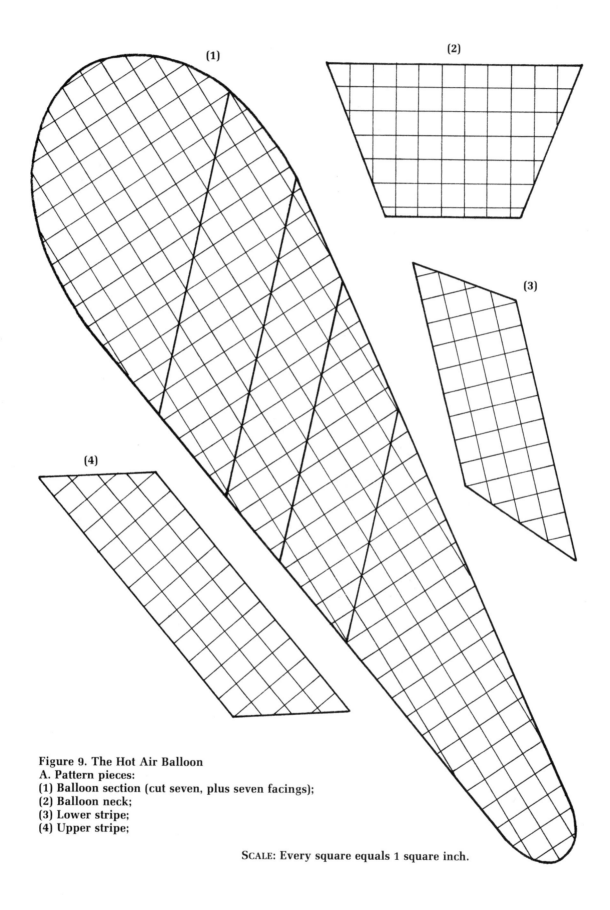

Figure 9. The Hot Air Balloon
A. Pattern pieces:
(1) Balloon section (cut seven, plus seven facings);
(2) Balloon neck;
(3) Lower stripe;
(4) Upper stripe;

SCALE: Every square equals 1 square inch.

Figure 9A. continued

(5)   (6)

(5) Gondola;
(6) Balloon mouth

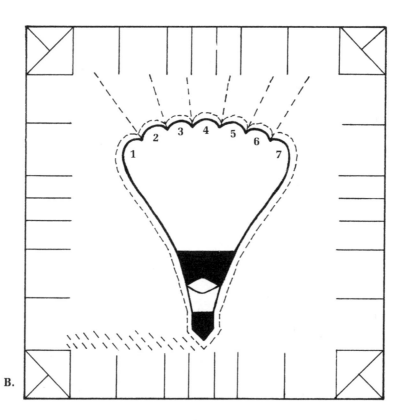

B.

B. The first row of quilt stitching (the solid black line) runs ¼ inch *inside* the outline of the balloon, around the neck, in straight lines between the bottom of the neck and the top of the gondola, and around the gondola. Broken black lines indicate the second row of quilt stitching, starting points for subsequent rows (lower left corner), and pivot lines (above the balloon). Quilt-stitch in concentric rings to the edge of the blue background. Then quilt-stitch over the seams between the border squares and the border rectangles. Quilt-stitch the *T*'s shown on the corner squares.

For balloon Sections 3 and 5, mark the stripes slanting upward as shown. For Sections 2, 4, and 6, turn the pattern over and mark the stripes through the pattern piece so that they will slant downward.

Reversible Playground Pals (QQQ)

Friendly animals—their faces on one side of the quilt, their tails on the other—seem to jump out of this cuddly comforter.

This quilt requires no scraps. You will need:

- a new flat twin solid-color sheet for the quilt top (Color **T**)
- a new flat twin sheet of another solid color for the quilt bottom (Color **B**)
- ½ yard of 60-inch-wide fabric for the teeter totter (see-saw)
- printed fabric for three small (5- to 8-inches-high) toy characters—cartoon characters, circus animals, etc.—*whose backs and fronts are not identical.* These fabrics are readily available at notions counters. They have seam lines and cutting lines already marked.
- printed fabric for one large (15- to 18-inches-high) toy character whose back and front are different
- approximately 1 yard of seam binding for the balloon string
- 1⅞ yards of trim for the jump rope
- 3¼ square yards of 8-ounce *bonded* polyester batting, and additional batting or pillow fill to stuff the toys and the balloon
- thread to match both sheets
- a sewing machine with a quilting guide, a size 9 or 11 (European size 65 or 75) needle, and a quilting foot
- a Bishop hem guide (Dritz® Ezy-Hem® Guide)
- an ironing board and an iron
- a point presser (optional)
- a yardstick
- pattern paper with a 1-inch grid
- approximately 70 large (1½-inch) safety pins (reusable)
- common pins
- a dark-colored washable marker
- a seam ripper

Using a seam ripper, remove the hems from the sheets. Then wash and dry them and the other fabrics by machine. Cut the top sheet to 76 × 56 inches. Lay it over the bottom sheet and align one of its corners with a corner of the bottom sheet. Smooth out wrinkles and safety-pin the sheets together on all sides. Using the top sheet as a guide, cut the bottom sheet to match. Save the scraps from the sheets to use as facings for the toys and the balloons.

Using the Bishop hem guide, press under ½ inch along both ends and one side of each sheet.

Sever a toy character's front piece from the other pieces on the fabric. You do not have to cut precisely around the outline of the toy. Lay the toy's front face down on the Color **T** scraps. With common pins perpendicular to the seam line, pin the top to the scrap. Stitch on the seam line, using a stitch-length setting of 16 (2 for metric machines). *Do not leave an opening.* On the cutting line, cut through both layers around the toy's outline. Clip the curves. On the Color **T** *facing only,* cut a horizontal slash to within ½ inch of each side. Turn the toy right side out through the slash. Use a point presser if necessary. Press the toy character flat. *Lightly* stuff the toy through the slash with bits of batting. Hand-stitch the slash closed. Sew each toy's front to a Color **T** facing and stuff it in this way.

Make the balloon by cutting a Color **B** circle 5½ inches in diameter and sewing it, *around the entire circumference,* to a Color **T** facing circle, with a ¼-inch (0.6-cm) seam. Clip the seam allowances. Cut a slash in the *facing* and turn the balloon right side out through the slash; press. Stuff the balloon lightly.

To make the pattern for the teeter-totter fulcrum, draw a line 9 inches long on pattern paper. Draw a perpendicular line 15 inches long above the center of the first line, bisecting it. With a straightedge or ruler, connect the ends of the 9-inch line to the end of the 15-inch line. Using this triangle as a pattern, cut two fulcrums for the teeter-totters. Cut two teeter-totter boards 55 inches long and 2 inches wide, and press under ¼ inch on all edges of the boards and the fulcrums. Set aside one fulcrum and one board to be used on the quilt bottom.

Drape the seam binding over the large toy character's right hand and baste the end onto the wrong side of the lower edge of the hand. Cut a 33-inch length of "jump rope" trim.

Lay the top pieces out on the quilt top sheet, using Figure 10 as a guide, and centering the pieces on an area 75 × 30 inches. Pull the seam binding over the large toy's hand, behind his head and about 8½ inches diagonally to the right. Do not cut the seam binding yet, but tuck the excess seam binding under the balloon. Position the rope-jumping character so that his hands cover the ends of the "rope." With the washable marker draw around all the pieces, the jump rope, and the seam binding.

Set aside the quilt-top pieces and lay the quilt-top sheet wrong side up on the floor. With unpressed selvage edges together, place the quilt bottom right side up over the quilt top. Safety-pin the two sheets together along all edges. With a washable marker trace the outlines from the quilt top onto the quilt bottom. Remove the pins.

Hand-baste the seam binding "balloon string" to the wrong side of the large toy's chin. Clip away the excess seam binding. On the quilt top, pin a length of seam binding over the outline between the character's head and the bottom of the balloon, allowing ½ inch extra at each end. Clip off the excess seam binding. Also pin the fulcrum, the teeter-totter board, and the jump rope in place.

Using a straight stitch, a stitch-length adjustment of 16 (2 for metric machines), and Color **T** top and bobbin threads, topstitch these pieces in place. Stitch along both edges of the seam binding and the "rope." Begin and end each seam by setting the stitch-length regulator temporarily on zero and taking three to five stitches in place.

With a measuring stick and a washable marker, draw lines that continue the top and bottom of the teeter-totter board out to the edges of the quilt top. These lines are the only quilt-stitching guidelines you will need to make.

Pin the toy characters and the balloon in place. Release the pressure on the presser foot slightly and topstitch them down.

Sew the toy characters' back pieces to Color **B** facings, clip the curves, cut slashes in the facings, and turn the toys right sides out. Make another balloon, this time using Color **T** for the right side and Color **B** for the facing.

On the quilt bottom, pin in place the fulcrum and the jump rope. Lay the seam binding inside its outline between the balloon and the large character's head; pull the lower end diagonally across the character's head. Tuck the end under the top of the character's shoulder and hand-baste it onto the wrong side. Hand-baste the seam binding onto the wrong side of the top of the character's head also. Snip away any excess seam binding and position it between the balloon and the head, allowing ½ inch excess at either end; pin. With the presser foot pressure on normal setting and the stitch length set for 16 (2 for metric machines), topstitch these pieces onto the sheet. Take three to five stitches in place at the beginnings and endings of seams.

Lay the characters, then the teeter-totter board, in position. With a washable marker, mark on the toys the areas where the board overlaps them. Lightly stuff the balloon and the toy characters, leaving unstuffed the areas to be obscured by the teeter-totter board. Pin the toys in place: they will be partly hidden by the board. Also pin the rope-jumping character onto the quilt's bottom sheet. Topstitch.

Pin and topstitch the teeter-totter board. Then pin and topstitch the characters (if any) not partially obscured by the board.

With right sides together, pin the unpressed edge of the quilt bottom to the unpressed edge of the quilt top. Sew a ½-inch (1.2-cm) seam and press the seam flat. Lay the quilt bottom face down on the floor. Cut the batting to 75 × 55 inches (it should touch the seam on the sewn edge and the folds on the other edges). Fold the quilt top over the batting. With common pins, secure the quilt top to the quilt bottom along the three unsewn edges. *Without lifting the quilt*, pin the three layers of the quilt together with well-spaced safety pins. *Don't* pin through the stuffed pieces.

Equip the sewing machine with Color **T** top thread, Color **B** bobbin thread, and set stitch length to 16 (2 for metric machines). Release the pressure on the presser foot slightly. With the quilt top on top, topstitch around the perimeter of the quilt, ⅛ inch from the outside.

To quilt, adjust the quilting guide attachment to 3 inches. Release the pressure on the presser foot slightly more. Use a stitch length of 9 (3 for metric machines), Color **T** top thread, and Color **B** bobbin thread. The first line of quilt stitching runs parallel to and 3 inches below the lower edge

Figure 10.   Reversible Playground Pals. Quilting (solid) lines run parallel to the top and bottom of the teeter-totter and the washable ink quilting guide lines (the broken lines).

of the teeter-totter board and its inked-on extensions (see Figure 10). Begin by placing a hand above and a hand below the quilt to smooth out wrinkles. Lower the needle and the presser foot. Take three to five stitches in place; then sew to the end of the quilting line, proceeding carefully and stopping periodically to smooth out wrinkles and to remove safety pins from your path. *Don't sew over safety pins.* Interrupt the quilting line ½ inch to the left and the right of the fulcrum. Finish the seam by taking three to five stitches in place.

Subsequent quilting lines run beneath and parallel to the first line. Do not quilt inside the arc of the jump rope: interrupt the quilting lines 1 inch outside the rope. Interrupt the line of quilt stitching where it comes within 1½ inches of the rope-jumping character. Quilt-stitch in parallel lines until you reach the lower edge of the quilt. Then begin quilt stitching on the upper half of the quilt by sewing a line parallel to the upper edge of the teeter-totter board and the washable ink lines. Interrupt the quilt-stitching lines 1½ inches from the stuffed toy characters. Quilt parallel lines to the upper edge of the quilt.

Clip threads. Follow the manufacturer's instructions to remove the washable ink. Dry alternately on permanent press and fluff cycles. Don't line dry or press this or any other quilt.

This Pal Is a PJs Pillow (QQ)

You can use "pal" fabric to make a child's pajama pillow. Have on hand:

- printed fabric for one large (15- to 18-inches-tall) toy character (see page 37 for further description)
- fabric to use as facings (approximately as much as the "pal" fabric)
- 4-ounce *bonded* polyester batting (same amount)
- fusible webbing (*not* interfacing)
- three snaps
- thread
- a point presser (optional)
- common pins
- an ironing board and an iron
- a sewing machine with a size 9 or 11 (European size 65 or 75) needle and a quilting foot

Prewash and dry the fabrics by machine.

Cut the printed fabric approximately in half between the toy's front and back; you don't have to cut precisely around the marked cutting line. Cut two facing and two batting pieces roughly the same dimensions as the toy's front and back pieces.

Lay a facing piece wrong side up. Over it, lay a segment of batting and then the toy's front fabric, right side up. Pin all three layers together around the perimeter. Loosen the presser-foot pressure slightly and, with a stitch length of 9 (3 for metric machines), sew on the outline marked stitching line. *Do not leave an opening;* sew all the way around the outline.

Quilt-stitch details: with toy fabric facing upward, merely topstitch over the printed lines delineating ears, eyes, tail, paws, jaw line, and other details as desired. Use the quilting foot. Begin each quilting line by setting the stitch-length adjustment temporarily on zero and taking three to five stitches in place. Use a stitch length of 9 (3 for metric machines) and the presser-foot pressure still in a slightly loosened position. Stitch in place at the end of each quilting line.

Lay the other facing wrong side up. Lay the batting and the toy's back fabric over it, right side up; pin and sew on the stitching line. Quilt-stitch details as desired.

Now cut all layers of front and back pieces on the marked cutting lines.

With right sides together, pin the toy's quilted back to the front. With a stitch length of 12 (2.5 for metric machines), sew on the stitching line. This time, don't sew the section marked

"Leave open for stuffing." Clip the curves and trim the seam allowances *except* at the opening. At the opening, trim away *all* of the *batting's* seam allowances but *none* of the *fabric's* seam allowances. Then, at the opening, machine straight-stitch the toy-front fabric's seam allowance to the seam allowance of the front facing. Use a stitch-length setting of 12 (2.5 for metric machines). Sew the back seam allowance to the back facing seam allowance.

Turn the pillow right side out. Use the point presser if necessary. Press the pillow flat, and press the seam allowances of the opening to the inside. Place fusible webbing strips between the seam allowances and the facings and press. Position the snaps along the seam allowances; hand-sew them.

Store nightclothes inside. The pillow is machine-washable on warm and gentle settings.

WARNING: This pillow may cause emotional attachment.

Real Pinwheel (QQ)

Normally, a queen-size quilt would be too large to quilt easily by machine, because half of the work must fit (or, more accurately, must *be made* to fit) between the needle and the vertical arm of the sewing machine. However, treating each quilt piece as an independent quilt and sewing large border pieces around a manageably small core make a large quilt—such as Real Pinwheel—possible.

Real Pinwheel is a slightly rectangular design, similar but not identical to the various traditional Windmill, Whirligig, and Pinwheel quilt blocks. You may show off its reversibility by using different fabrics on top and bottom. You will need to buy cotton with a smooth, tight weave in the following amounts:

- 50 inches, or 25 inches if the fabric is at least 50 inches wide, for the **A** pieces on the quilt top
- 50 inches, or 25 inches if the fabric is at least 50 inches wide, for the bottom **A** pieces
- 2 square yards for the quilt top's **B** pieces
- 2 square yards for the quilt bottom's **B** pieces
- 1½ yards at least 50 inches wide for the quilt top's **C** and **D** pieces
- 1½ yards at least 50 inches wide for the quilt bottom's **C** and **D** pieces

You will also need:

- a full-size flat sheet for the **E** and **F** top pieces
- a full-size flat sheet for the **E** and **F** bottom pieces
- 9½ square yards of 5-ounce *bonded* polyester batting
- 12½ yards of quilt binding
- a zigzag sewing machine with a 6-inch quilting guide, a size 9 or 11 (European size 65 or 75) needle, and a quilting foot
- a point presser (optional)
- an ironing board and an iron
- thread
- two flat, non-shank clear buttons at least ¾ inch in diameter
- a yardstick
- pattern paper with a 1-inch grid
- pattern weights
- a T square
- a straightedge
- a compass
- 50 or so large (1½-inch) safety pins (reusable)
- common pins
- a washable marker

Prewash and dry fabrics and sheets in a machine.

You will need to make only two pattern pieces for this quilt: the **C/D** piece and the **E/F** piece. To make the **A** fabric triangles, simply cut the **A** fabric into two 25-inch squares. Fold and pin the squares in half diagonally (for striped fabric, refer to the cutting scheme in Figure 11A), press the fold lines, and cut on the resulting creases. For the **B** pieces, start with two 35⅓-inch squares. Fold them diagonally, press, and cut on the creases.

Refer to Figure 11A as you proceed to make the **C/D** and **E/F** pattern pieces.

To make pattern piece **C**, draw a line 12⅞ inches long. Draw perpendicular lines 41½ and 29¼ inches long, respectively, to the right of the top and bottom ends of the first line. Connect the end of the 41½-inch line to the end of the 29¼-inch line. Label this **C**, but don't cut the piece out yet.

For **D**, extend piece **C**'s 29¼-inch-long line **C** another 8⅛ inches. Place the point of a compass on the end of the 41½-inch line and construct a circle with a radius of 6⅓ inches. Connect the ends of the 41½-inch and the 37-inch lines by situating a T square so that it touches the ends of both lines when the T square's corner is on the circumference of the circle. Label this pattern piece **D** and cut out the **C/D** pattern piece.

Make pattern piece **E** by drawing a line 80 inches long at least 5⅞ inches away from the lower edge of the pattern paper. At each end draw lines at 45-degree angles, using the grid on the pattern paper as a guide. The line on the left is 17 inches long; the one on the right is 29¼ inches long. Make a right angle at the end of the line on the right edge, using the T square, and draw a 12⅓-inch line at a right angle to the line on the right edge. Connect the end of this new line to the end of the 17-inch line, forming a line parallel to the original 80-inch line and 18 inches away. Label this piece **E**, but don't cut it out yet.

For pattern piece **F**, continue the line on the lower right edge of piece **E** to the edge of the paper. Draw a line parallel to and 5⅞ inches distant from the original 80-inch line of piece **E**. Create a right angle at the left end of this new line; connect its end to the left end of the original 80-inch line. Label this extension **F** and cut out the **E/F** pattern piece.

Before cutting the rest of the fabric, cut out the batting pieces. Begin by forming a 116 × 105-inch rectangle of batting; hand-baste batting segments together without overlapping them. Then, beginning at a corner with the **F** pattern piece, draw around the pattern pieces with the washable ink marker, according to the layout scheme suggested by the finished quilt (see Figure 11B). However, remember that although there is plenty of batting in the rectangle, there will be some gaps between the pieces, because the pattern pieces contain seam allowances and the finished quilt pieces do not. Use fabric triangles in place of pattern pieces for batting pieces **A** and **B**. Cut four pieces **A**, four **B**, two **C**, two **D**, two **E**, and two **F** from the batting.

Cut out fabric pieces **C**, **D**, **E**, and **F**, using pattern pieces *right side up for the quilt's top pieces* and *wrong side up for the quilt's bottom pieces*. To cut the **E** pieces, fold up the **F** extension on the original 80-inch line. Fold the extension down to cut the **F** pieces. Similarly, fold the **D** extension up to cut the **C** pieces, and down to cut the **D** pieces.

Construct each segment as a separate quilt. Pin a quilt top **A** piece to a quilt bottom **A** piece with right sides together. Lay an **A** batting piece over the pinned fabric triangles; remove the pins one at a time, replacing them through all three layers. With a stitch length of 9 (3 for metric machines) and the presser-foot pressure slightly loosened, the batting lying against the throat plate and the fabric facing upward, sew a ¼-inch (0.6-cm) seam around the edge; leave a 10-inch opening in the middle of the hypotenuse (the long edge). Trim the batting almost to the seam line at the corners. Clip the fabric at the corners. Fold in the edges of the opening ¼ inch; press and pin. Turn the segment right side out through the opening and press it flat along the seams. Topstitch the opening closed. Do likewise for the remaining three **A** segments.

Construct the **B** segments the same way, leaving 10-inch openings in the hypotenuses and topstitching them closed after the **B** triangles have been clipped, trimmed, and pressed. Seg-

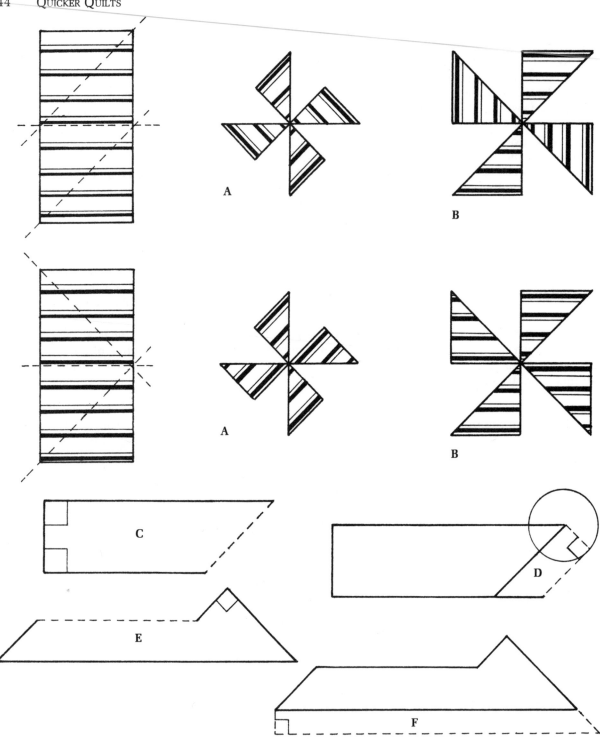

Figure 11.   Real Pinwheel.
A. *(Top row)* **Cutting the right-triangle pieces A and B according to this scheme yields two pairs of triangles with stripes parallel to each other's, but not to those of the other pair. Another cutting scheme** *(second row)* **yields all parallel-striped pieces.** *(Third and fourth rows)* **The construction of pattern pieces C/D and E/F.**

Figure 11 continued

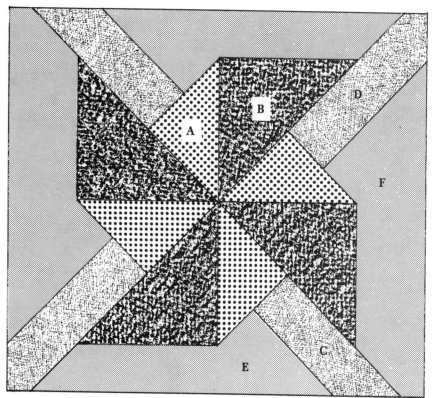

B. To prevent the wasting of batting, first hand-lace batting lengths together with long hand stitches to form a 116 × 105-inch rectangle. Then cut out the pieces, using this as a layout guide. Begin by laying the F pattern piece over the batting at a corner. Hold the paper pattern in place with pattern weights and draw around it with the washable marker. Next draw around the pieces bordering the F piece. Draw around the remaining pattern pieces. Cut on the lines. If you must cut through the threads, immediately tie knots in the severed thread ends.

ments **C**, **D**, **E**, and **F** involve no such topstitching; simply leave unsewn edges that will form the border of the quilt (see Figure 11B).

To quilt each **A** segment, set the quilt-guide attachment for 6 inches and the stitch-length adjustment for 9 (3 for metric machines). Leave the presser-foot pressure slightly loosened. Quilt-stitch a smaller triangle 6 inches inside the edges of the **A** segment. Begin and end the quilting by temporarily putting the stitch-length adjustment on zero and taking three to five stitches in place. Note that the interior triangle formed by quilting is *much* smaller than the **A** segment.

Before quilting the **B** segments, use a few large safety pins to secure all three layers together and prevent shifting (see Figure 11C). Quilt-stitch a smaller triangle 6 inches inside each **B** segment. Remove any safety pins in your path; *don't try to stitch over safety pins.*

Safety pins aren't necessary for segments **C** and **D**. Simply set the quilt-guide attachment for 3 inches and quilt-stitch one row parallel to each long edge. Stitch in place at the beginning and end of every row of quilt stitching.

For quilt-stitching **E** and **F** segments, use safety pins to prevent the layers from shifting. Return the quilting-guide attachment to the 6-inch setting, and sew in rows parallel to the long edges, *beginning at the inward (pointed) edge.* If one of the sheets is striped, you may be able to

Figure 11 *continued*

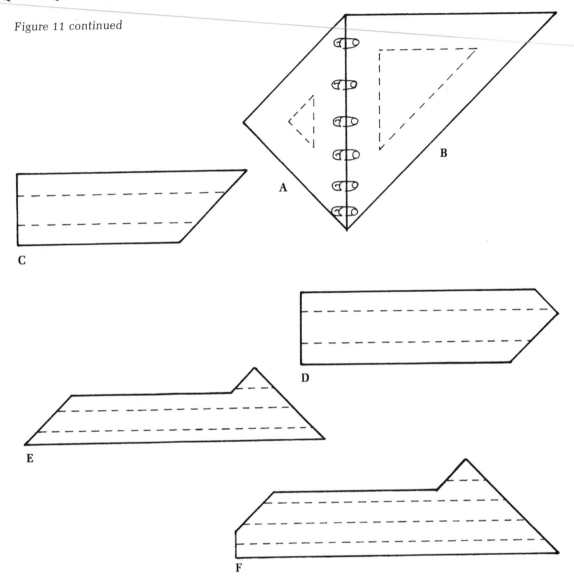

C. (Above): An A segment is "basted" with safety pins to a B segment before the two are satin-stitched together. Notice the quilting lines. (Below): Quilting lines for segments C, D, E, and F.

follow the stripes; otherwise, you will have to use the washable marker to delineate the first and second rows of quilt stitching. In either case, each row of quilt stitching serves as a guide for the next row.

To join these "mini-quilts" together, begin at the center. Lay an **A** segment against a **B** segment without overlapping them. With large safety pins "baste" segment **A** to segment **B**. Then satin-stitch them together carefully on the sewing machine, removing the pins before you get to them; leave the presser-foot pressure slightly loosened. Using the zigzag presser foot, a stitch length of 20 (0.5 for metric machines), and the widest zigzag stitch, sew a segment **A** to a segment **B**. To prevent the machine from jamming, hold the excess top thread in your hand and pull it taut toward the back of the sewing machine as you take three to five stitches in place and a few stitches forward. Baste with safety pins and sew together all segments **A** and **B**. Don't try to sew over safety pins.

NOTE: There will be a hole as big around as a pencil in the center of the core of **A** and **B** triangles.

Then join each segment **E** to a segment **C**, and each segment **F** to a segment **D**. Sew these border segments to the center core of **A**'s and **B**'s, starting in the center and working toward the outside. Then sew the remaining seams between the **C**'s and the **F**'s, and the **D**'s and the **E**'s.

Sew the two flat, non-shank clear buttons over the hole in the center where **A**'s and **B**'s come together. Thread a needle with 18 inches of doubled thread. With one button below the quilt and one above, push the needle through an eye of the lower button and an eye of the upper button, pulling only half of the thread through. Continue to sew the buttons together. On the lower side of the quilt, pull the "non-needle" end of the thread through to the wrong side of the button; make loops and knots around the button and sever the thread. Take several more stitches through the buttons' eyes and then knot and clip the thread.

Encase the outside edges in quilt binding. Pin the binding on, mitering the corners (see page 7). Then, with the presser-foot pressure still slightly loosened and the stitch-length adjustment set for 12 (2.5 for metric machines), straight-stitch ¼ inch and ⅛ inch from the inside edge of the quilt binding.

Clip threads. Follow the manufacturer's instructions for removing washable marker lines. Machine-wash on a warm and gentle cycle. Dry alternately on timed warm and fluff cycles. For best results use a large commercial machine.

A Doll Quilt (QQQQ)

This cuddly quilt features ruffled binding and a hood. To make it you will need:

- 1 square yard of a print fabric
- 1 square yard of another print fabric
- 1 square yard of 3- or 3.3-ounce bonded polyester batting
- thread
- 2¾ yards of ruffled quilt binding
- a sewing machine with a quilting guide attachment, a size 9 or 11 (European size 65 or 75) needle, and a quilting foot
- a Bishop hem guide (Dritz® Ezy-Hem® Guide)
- a yardstick
- pattern paper
- a washable ink marker
- about 40 large (1½-inch) safety pins (reusable)
- common pins
- fabric shears
- a seam ripper

Prewash and dry fabric.

Cut a 27 × 21-inch rectangle from each fabric and from the batting. Lay one fabric rectangle wrong side up on a flat surface. Over it lay the batting, and then the other fabric rectangle, right side up. Secure all three layers together with safety pins—two at each corner and the rest distributed throughout the rest of the quilt.

Set the quilting guide attachment for 1½ inches. Set the stitch-length regulator for 9 (3 for metric machines) and loosen the presser-foot pressure very slightly. Align the quilting guide with the raw edge of the fabric at a corner, lower the needle into the cloth, and, with the stitch-length adjustment temporarily on zero, take three to five stitches in place. Quilt the first row parallel to, and 1½ inches from, a 27-inch-long side of the quilt (see Figure 12A). *Remove safety pins in your path.* Stop, with the needle in the fabric, 1½ inches from the end of the quilt. Pivot the quilt 90 degrees and align the quilting guide with the edge of the quilt. Sew a row of quilt stitching 1½ inches from the edge of the quilt, stopping 1½ inches from the end. Pivot again and sew 1½ inches from the edge of the third side of the quilt to 1½ inches from the end. Pivot and sew to 1½ inches of the first row of quilt stitching. Now align the quilting-guide attachment with the last parallel row of quilting. Stop and pivot 1½ inches before the corner. Continue in this way until the center unquilted portion of the quilt is narrower than 3 inches. Finish the quilt stitching by setting the stitch-length adjustment on zero and taking three to five stitches in place.

Make the pattern for the hood by drawing a 10-inch line on the pattern paper. At one end of the line draw another, perpendicular to the first line and 10 inches long. Connect the ends of the two lines to form a triangle. Cut one such triangle from each print of fabric and one from the batting.

Use common pins to pin the batting triangle to the *wrong* side of one of the fabric triangles.

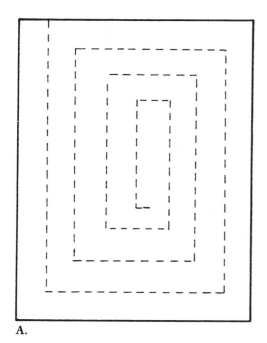

A.

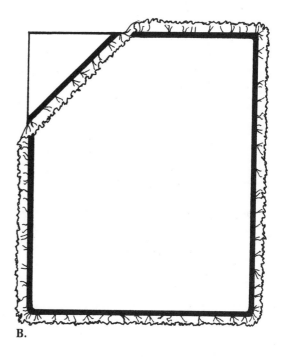

B.

Figure 12.   A Doll Quilt.
A. The quilt-stitching lines.
B. **Encase the raw edges of the rectangle and the raw edges of the hood in one continuous length of ruffled quilt binding.**

Leaving the presser-foot pressure slightly loosened and setting the stitch length for 6 (4 for metric machines), baste the batting to the fabric along all three edges, with the batting facing downward.

Then lay the rectangle on a flat surface with the fabric matching the batted triangle facing upward. Align the right-angle corner of the batted triangle with a corner of the rectangle—right sides together—and pin with common pins along the two outside edges. On the other side of the quilt, lay the remaining fabric triangle over the same corner, with right sides together. Remove the pins one at a time and replace them—from the unbatted side of the hood—through all three layers.

Sew, with a stitch length of 12 (2.5 for metric machines), with the presser-foot pressure still very slightly loosened, and with the batting facing downward. Begin at the corner and sew down the sides, one at a time. Reinforce the seam by sewing again over the line of stitching. Clip and trim the corner. Then turn the unbatted triangle right side out.

To facilitate applying the ruffled quilt binding, round off the rectangle's three corners. Lay the round corner of the Bishop hem guide over each corner; draw around the hem guide's corner with the washable marker. Cut on the line.

Beginning in the middle of one side of the rectangle, encase the raw edges of the rectangle and the raw edges of the hood in one continuous length of ruffled quilt binding (see Figure 12B); pin. At the finish, cut the end at least ½ inch beyond the beginning of the pinned end. Use a seam ripper to undo the binding's topstitching just far enough to turn the raw edge under ¼ inch; press. Pin the pressed end over the beginning end so that the beginning end is encased inside it. Topstitch, with a stitch length of 12 (2.5 for metric machines) and the presser-foot pressure still slightly loosened, twice around the perimeter of the quilt, ⅛ and ¼ inch from the edge, and over the pressed edge of the end of the binding.

That's all there is to it. Follow the manufacturer's instructions for removing washable ink lines, or launder this quilt on warm and gentle cycles; never press or line-dry it.

Variation: A Baby Quilt (QQQQ)

The Doll Quilt is big enough for a real—newborn—baby. You can make a baby quilt from the Doll Quilt directions, or you can vary those directions by making the rectangle large enough to wrap an older baby. To do so, buy 4 yards of ruffled quilt binding, 1½ square yards of batting, and 1 yard each of two different fabrics that are at least 46 inches wide after preshrinking. Cut the hood pattern the same size as for the Doll Quilt, but make the "rectangle" 36 inches square. Use the quilt-stitching pattern and the sewing instructions given for the Doll Quilt.

Variation: A Doll Quilt from Prequilted Fabric (QQQQ)

Using prequilted fabric will, of course, save time. You won't need batting. Just buy 1 square yard of double-faced, prequilted material, and, for the hood, ⅓ yard of ordinary fabric. Allow for preshrinking. You may be able to find unquilted fabric that matches the prequilted material. Or, choose something interesting from a remnant bin or your own scrap bag.

Cut the rectangle and one triangle piece from the prequilted fabric; cut the other triangle from the unquilted material.

Omit the quilt stitching.

Decide which side of the prequilted triangular hood fabric you want to show. Lay that side face down over the matching side of the rectangle; pin. On the other side of the quilt, lay the unquilted fabric triangle over the same corner of the rectangle, with right sides together. Remove the pins one at a time and replace them through all three layers. Sew. Add ruffled quilt binding, following the instructions in "A Doll Quilt," page 49.

Variation: A Baby Quilt from Prequilted Fabric (QQQQ)

Buy no batting, but purchase 4 yards of ruffled quilt binding, 1 yard of double-faced, prequilted fabric that is at least 46 inches wide after preshrinking, and ⅓ yard of ordinary, unquilted material. Cut the "rectangle" 36 inches square. Then follow the instructions for "A Doll Quilt from Prequilted Fabric," above.

Cabin Fever. This design is inspired by the traditional Log Cabin quilt block. It can be constructed with a solid backing or in pairs of three-layer units that make the quilt reversible and eliminate the problem of managing the quilt stitching of a large quilt on a regular sewing machine.

Kaleido'Scraps. Quilt blocks can be "extended" by spacing them with blocks of either a solid, complementary color or an imaginative print — here, red bandannas.

Baby Dragons. The squares made of contrasting triangles can be turned in different directions to create very different quilt top designs. Try different arrangements before sewing.

Baby Dragons, *reverse.* This quilt back is constructed with only a few pieces, yet it succeeds on its own as a design, making Baby Dragons reversible.

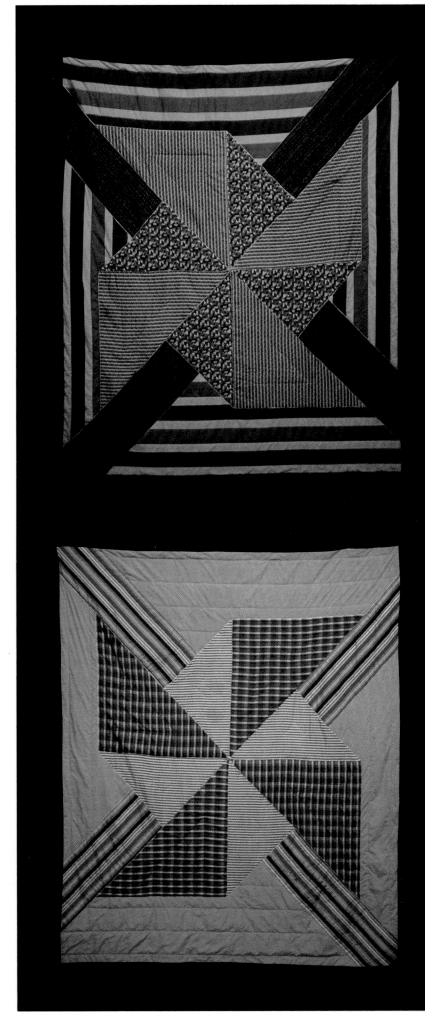

Real Pinwheel. Striped fabric makes a dramatic setting for the bold center pattern.

Real Pinwheel, *reverse.* Each unit in this design is stuffed and quilted individually. Then these "miniquilts" are assembled to make the overall pattern.

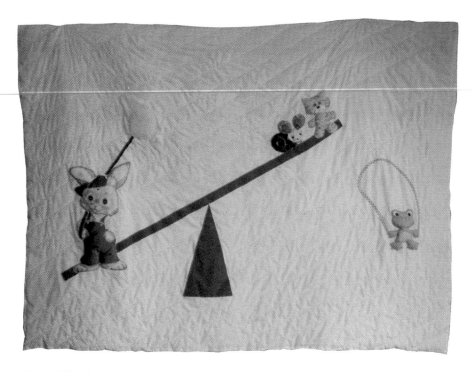

Reversible Playground Pals. This quilt incorporating novelty fabric prints of the fronts and backs of the same whimsical animal characters will delight children.

Stained Glass Window Quilt. Streamlined construction methods and bias tape make an intricate-looking design easy to execute.

Hot Air Balloon. Stuffing with batting or pillow fill gives this quilt another dimension.

Doll's Quilt. This very easy quilt is actually large enough for a newborn baby.

Baby Butterfly. A single image reverse-appliquéd to a contrasting background makes a dramatic baby quilt that can be completed quickly.

Maple Log Cabin. This quilt, like Cabin Fever, is simply an enlarged version of a Log Cabin block. It too can be made reversible by adding pairs of three-layer units to the center panel. The center motif is reverse-appliquéd.

Six Moons of Saturn. This is an eyecatching contemporary quilt with matching pillow shams. The oval quilting lines suggest the moons' orbits.

Six Moons of Saturn, *detail*. Trapunto and cording provide unusual texture in this fabric painting.

Border-Print Bedspread. Following the cutting layouts carefully and adding the piping are the secrets of this easy quilted bedspread.

Border-Print Bedspread, *pillow shams.* Matching pillow shams with coordinated ruffles echo the quilting design of the bedspread.

Granddaughter's Flower Garden. A block of traditional Grandmother's Flower Garden suggested the idea for this quilt. Here, the design is unified by the color arrangement and by the use of striped fabric for the first ring of hexagons. See the reverse side of this quilt on the back jacket.

Woven Coverlet. Varying the weave changes the look of this fascinating reversible quilt. Compare the woven coverlet in the front jacket photograph.

Woven Coverlet, *patchwork pillow.* This "woven-look" patchwork pillow mimics the texture of the coverlet, but it is actually made of simple patchwork squares with quilt stitching like the coverlet's.

Maple Log Cabin (QQQ)

This design incorporates a relatively new part of Canada's heritage into an older tradition: the Log Cabin patchwork block. Like Cabin Fever, the Maple Log Cabin coverlet is a single 83¾ × 77¼-inch block, rather than a pattern of dozens of blocks. The central maple leaf is created with an easy machine reverse-appliqué technique. The same line of stitching around the maple leaf's outline does the appliquéing and the quilt stitching simultaneously.

You will need:

- a red flat twin sheet
- an off-white (not white) flat twin sheet (white looks too much like a bed sheet)
- a flat, full-size, off-white sheet for the quilt bottom
- 5½ square yards of 4-ounce bonded polyester batting
- off-white and red thread
- fusible webbing (not interfacing)
- a sewing machine with a size 9 or 11 (European size 65 or 75) needle and a quilting foot
- a Bishop hem guide (Dritz® Ezy-Hem® Guide)
- an ironing board and an iron
- a yardstick
- a French curve
- pattern paper with 1-inch grid
- pattern weights
- masking tape
- 80 or so large (1½-inch) safety pins (reusable)
- common pins
- fabric shears
- a seam ripper
- a washable marker

Remove the hems from the sheets. Prewash (separately) and dry them by machine. Cut a 16¾ × 14¼-inch rectangle from a corner of the off-white twin sheet, two identical rectangles from a corner of the red sheet, and one such rectangle from a corner of the batting.

Draft the maple leaf pattern to scale on the pattern paper (Figure 13A). *Don't cut around the outline of the leaf.* Fold the pattern paper in half on the leaf's dotted center line. Using an unthreaded sewing machine and a stitch length of 9 (3 for metric machines), "sew" over the maple leaf's outline through both layers of paper.

To transfer the maple leaf image onto the off-white rectangle, begin by folding the rectangle in half lengthwise, pinning it, and pressing in a center crease. Lay the paper pattern over the fabric rectangle, aligning the dotted center line with the crease of the fabric and holding the pattern piece in place with pattern weights. Trace repeatedly over the perforated outline with the washable marking pen.

Thread the sewing machine with off-white thread. Begin stitching over the outline of the leaf by putting the stitch-length adjustment temporarily on zero and taking three to five stitches in place. Using a stitch length of 16 (2 for metric machines), sew around the outline; take three to

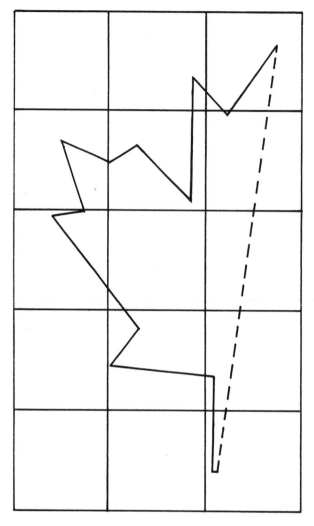

Figure 13.   Maple Log Cabin.
A. Draft the maple leaf pattern piece. Each square equals 3 square inches. Don't cut on the outline, but fold the pattern on the dotted line and perforate it with an unthreaded sewing machine.

five stitches in place to finish. Trim away the fabric *inside* the leaf outline to within ½ inch of the seam line; clip corners to the seam. Press the ½-inch seam allowance to the *inside* (Figure 13B). Lay strips of fusible webbing between the seam allowances and the wrong side of the off-white sheet; press again.

Lay the off-white rectangle right side up over a red rectangle, also right side up; pin with common pins around the leaf outline. Lay the batting rectangle over the remaining red rectangle; lay the pinned rectangles right side up over the batting. Remove the pins one at a time and replace them through all four layers. Use a few safety pins to secure all the layers together. Loosen the presser-foot pressure slightly. Using off-white thread and a stitch length of 16 (2 for metric machines), topstitch and quilt simultaneously by sewing around the maple leaf on the off-white fabric, as close to the edge as possible. Begin and end by stitching in place. Remove pins. *Without cutting the off-white fabric*, trim the other three layers even with the off-white seam allowance.

Figure 13 continued

B. After stitching around the leaf's outline on the off-white rectangle, trim away the fabric *inside* **the outline, leaving a ½-inch (1.2-cm) seam allowance. Clip to the corners as shown. Notice that the maple leaf has been positioned along the rectangle's center crease (the broken lines).**

All remaining pieces, except the two border strips, are 6¾ inches wide. Cut 6¾-inch-wide strips from both the red and the off-white twin sheets, lengthwise. Make the side panels of the Canadian flag from one such red strip: pin one end of the strip to a side of the maple leaf rectangle, right sides together; cut off the excess, pin the excess to the other wide of the rectangle, and again sever the excess. Sew, using a stitch length of 12 (2.5 for metric machines) and a ¼-inch

Figure 13 continued

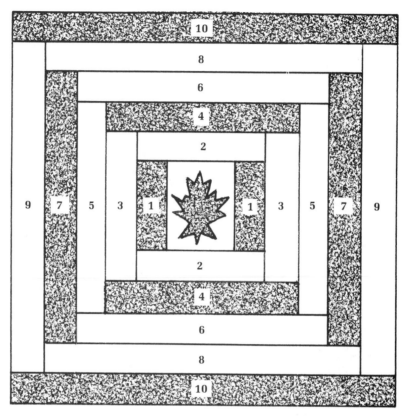

C. Sew the panels around the center core in the sequence indicated by the numbers.

(0.6-cm) seam. Press the seam allowances open. Now sew on the top and bottom off-white panels. Continue adding side panels, then top and bottom panels, using Figure 13C as a guide. *All seams are ¼ inch (0.6 cm).* Press seam allowances open before adding the next pair of panels.

To make the side borders, cut red strips 2¼ inches wide; piece them together, if necessary, to form two 2¼-inch-wide strips at least ½ inch longer than the sides of the quilt. Press one end of each strip under ¼ inch. Press in a lengthwise fold, 1 inch from an edge of each strip, with right sides out. Set aside.

Pin the full-size off-white sheet in half lengthwise, right sides together, and press in a crease. Remove the pins. Pin this sheet to an end of the quilt top, beginning at both edges and working toward the center crease. Use a washable marker to record the amount of excess sheet-width by marking points on both sides of the beginning of the excess of the sheet fabric (see Figure 13D). Unpin from quilt top. Fold and pin the sheet along the crease again with right sides together, pinning sparingly. Place the sheet on the sewing machine with the needle inserted through one of the washable ink marks and with the excess sheet fabric to the right of the needle. Use a strip of masking tape to mark the placement of the crease on the bed of the sewing machine. This will serve as a seam-width guide (see Figure 13E). Set the stitch length for 12 (2.5 for metric machines), align the crease with the edge of the masking tape, and sew the *length* of the sheet. Trim the tuck to ½ inch from the seam and press the seam allowances open.

With right sides together, pin and sew an end of the sheet to the upper edge of the quilt top, using a ¼-inch (0.6-cm) seam and a stitch-length setting of 12 (2.5 for metric machines). Press the

Figure 13 continued

D. Fold the bottom sheet in half lengthwise and press in a crease. Pin the sheet to the quilt top, beginning at the outside edges and working toward the center. Use a washable marker on both sides of the sheet's fold to mark the beginning of the excess portion of the sheet.

seam allowances open; then fold the two layers together on the seam line and press again. Press the edge of the opposite end of the quilt top under ¼ inch, using the Bishop hem guide. Pin the borders to the sides of the quilt top: align the folds in the ends of the borders with the seam connecting the quilt top with the quilt bottom, and pin the narrower "half" of each border to the quilt top, right sides together. Sew the borders to the quilt top with ¼-inch (0.6 cm) seams and a stitch length of 12 (2.5 for metric machines). Press the seam allowances open. At the lower end of the quilt top, trim the borders so that they extend only ¼ inch beyond the end of the quilt top. Press the border ends under ¼ inch.

Place the quilt top wrong side up on the floor. Smooth out any wrinkles. Cut and piece the batting to conform exactly to the quilt top's dimensions. It should touch the seam line at the top edge, the fold at the bottom edge, and the folds at the side border edges. Fold the border bottoms over the batting. Then fold the quilt bottom sheet down over the batting. Place a few safety pins at the upper edge to prevent the quilt from curling. Use common pins to pin the selvage edges of the bottom sheet over the border bottoms. Trim the bottom edge of the quilt bottom about ½ inch longer than the fold at the lower edge of the quilt top. Manually fold the quilt bottom's lower edge under ½ inch and pin it to the quilt top. *Without lifting the quilt,* distribute large safety pins throughout the quilt to secure all three layers together.

Sew the quilt bottom to the borders by topstitching with a stitch length of 16 (2 for metric machines) over the selvage edges of the sheet—as close to the edges as possible. Begin and end this topstitching by stitching in place with the stitch-length regulator temporarily on zero.

To do the quilt stitching, simply sew over the seams between the panels—but not over the

Figure 13 continued

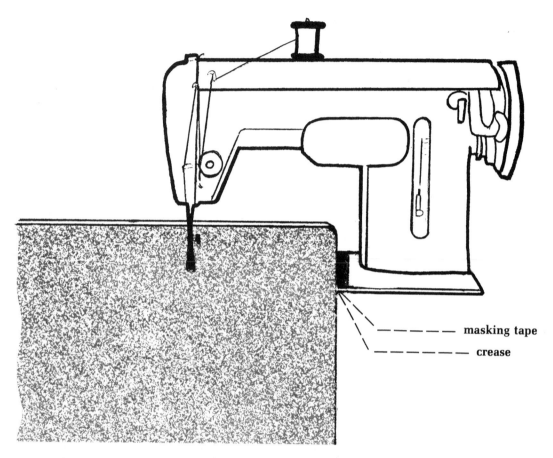

_ _ _ _ _ _ _ — **masking tape**

_ _ _ _ _ _ _ — **crease**

E. Insert the needle through the washable ink mark, with the excess sheet fabric to the right of the needle. Then use a strip of masking tape to mark the placement of the crease on the bed of the sewing machine. The masking tape will serve as a seam-width guide when you sew the sheet's center seam.

topstitching around the maple leaf. Release the pressure on the presser foot slightly. Lower the needle into an end of the seam between the maple leaf's rectangle and one of the first red (flag) panels. With the stitch-length setting temporarily on zero, take three to five stitches in place. Place one hand above and one below the quilt to smooth out wrinkles along the seam line. Then, with a stitch length of 9 (3 for metric machines), sew to the end of the seam line, removing safety pins as you come to them. *Don't try to sew over safety pins.* Take another three to five stitches in place at the end of the seam line. Quilt-stitch over the remaining seams, starting in the middle of the quilt and working toward the outside. Begin and end each quilt-stitching line by taking three to five stitches in place. Proceed carefully, and remember periodically to place hands above and below the quilt to smooth out wrinkles. When the quilt stitching has been done over all the seams, use red thread to quilt-stitch a row 1 inch from the edges of the upper and lower ends (the non-border edges) of the quilt. Then topstitch around the entire perimeter, ⅛ inch (0.3 cm) from the edge.

To remove ink marks, follow the manufacturer's instructions. If none are specified, machine-wash and dry on warm and gentle cycles. Do not line-dry or press this or any other quilt.

Variation: Three Layers Constructed Simultaneously (Q)

This variation has Maple Log Cabin on the quilt top and Cabin Fever on the reverse.

The technique of adding the three layers—top, bottom, and batting—simultaneously eliminates the need for quilting. This allows you to add more pairs of panels to the Maple Log Cabin design if you want a quilt larger than 83¾ × 77¼ inches. Buy larger sheets for the quilt top if necessary.

Make the quilt top's center rectangle as directed in Maple Log Cabin; use 3- or 4-ounce bonded batting for the maple leaf. For the rest of the quilt you may want to use heavier bonded batting. Cut batting and a center rectangle for the quilt bottom the same size as the maple leaf rectangle.

Lay the batting over the *wrong* side of the quilt bottom's center rectangle, and lay the maple leaf rectangle *right* side up over the batting. Pin along all four edges. With the presser-foot pressure slightly loosened, use a size 14 (European size 90) needle and a stitch length of 6 (4 for metric machines) to baste around the perimeter, ¼ inch (0.6 cm) from the edge.

The pairs of quilt top, quilt bottom, and batting panels are added in the same manner as in Variation: Reversible Cabin Fever, using the technique of adding three layers simultaneously (see page 19). However, because the top of this quilt is the Maple Log Cabin design, *all panels in this quilt are 6¾ inches wide.*

Cut fabric for the first (red) quilt top panel 6¾ inches wide. Pin it to one edge of the center rectangle and trim it to the proper length. Use this panel as a pattern to cut the second red panel, the bottom's first pair of panels, and two pieces of batting.

Pin the panels of the quilt bottom to opposite edges of the quilt bottom's center rectangle, right sides together. Lay the batting over the bottom panels, remove the pins one at a time, and replace them through all the layers. Turn the quilt over. On the quilt top, lay the red panels over the pinned edges of the center rectangle, with right sides together; pin. Turn the quilt over and remove all the pins with heads on the quilt bottom.

Sew, using a size 14 (European size 90) needle, a quilting foot, a stitch length of 12 (2.5 for metric machines), and a ¼-inch (0.6-cm) seam, *with the batting facing downward.* Leave the presser-foot pressure slightly loosened. You won't need to press the seams or trim the seam allowances (but if the batting's seam allowances exceed the fabric's ¼-inch (0.6-cm) seam allowances, trim the batting even with the other seam allowances). Before proceeding to the next step, make sure that all layers have been caught in the seam.

Cut off-white fabric for the next pair of quilt-top panels 6¾ inches wide. Before pinning the fabric to an edge of the center rectangle and the ends of the first pair of panels, pin the ends of the first pair of panels through top, batting, and bottom layers; this will keep the ends square. Cut the off-white fabric to the proper length; unpin it. Then cut the other off-white panel, the batting, and the second pair of quilt-bottom panels, using the first off-white panel as a pattern.

Pin the bottom panels to the opposite ends of the center rectangle and the ends of the first pair of sewn panels, with right sides together. Lay the batting over the bottom panels, remove the pins one at a time, and replace them through all the layers. Turn the quilt over. On the quilt top, lay the quilt-top's panel over the pinned edges of the center rectangle and the ends of the first pair of sewn (red) panels, with right sides together; pin. Turn the quilt bottom over and remove all the pins with heads on the quilt bottom.

Sew, with the batting facing downward against the throat plate of the sewing machine. Trim the seam allowance of the batting if it looks excessive. Before proceeding to the next step, make sure that all layers have been caught in the seam.

Continue adding pairs of panels (Figure 14A) until the quilt is the desired size. The sequence

Figure 14.   Maple Log Cabin Variation.
A. **Add pairs of panels (top, bottom, and batting) until the quilt is as big as you want it. On the Maple Log Cabin side of the quilt, the sequence is: two pairs of off-white panels, one pair of red panels, two pairs of off-white panels, one pair of red, etc.**

   One line of stitching serves as both seam and quilting. Sew with the batting facing downward against the throat plate.

for the Maple Log Cabin side is: two pairs of off-white panels, one pair of red panels, two pairs of off-white panels, one pair of red panels, etc. *All seams are ¼-inch (0.6-cm).* Remember to check each seam before adding the next pair of panels.

There is no quilt stitching.

Encase the raw edges of the last panels in the red sheet material, as follows: Cut 3-inch-wide strips on the grain of the fabric. Piece strips together, if necessary for length, with ¼-inch (0.6-cm) seams; press these seams open. Along a long edge use the Bishop hem guide to press ½ inch (1.2 cm) to the wrong side. Then press in what will become the center crease, 1 inch above the first fold line. See Figure 14B. Pin the unpressed long edge of the strip to the two side edges of the quilt, right sides together. Sew a ½-inch (1.2-cm) seam with a stitch length of 12 (2.5 for metric machines). Don't press the seam—simply fold the binding on the center crease and pin the folded edge to the quilt bottom. Topstitch along the folded edge with a stitch length of 12 (2.5 for metric machines).

Before pinning the binding to the quilt's upper and lower edges, press under ½ inch (1.2 cm) at one end of the remaining two lengths of binding. Pin the unpressed long edge of each length of binding to an end of the quilt and the ends of the side bindings, right sides together, beginning at the pressed end. Finger-press the unpressed raw end to the inside. Sew, using a ½-inch (1.2-cm) seam. Fold the binding on the center crease and topstitch over the folded edge. Topstitch closed the open corner edges.

Follow the manufacturer's instructions for removing washable ink marks. Dry the quilt alternately on warm and fluff settings.

Figure 14 continued

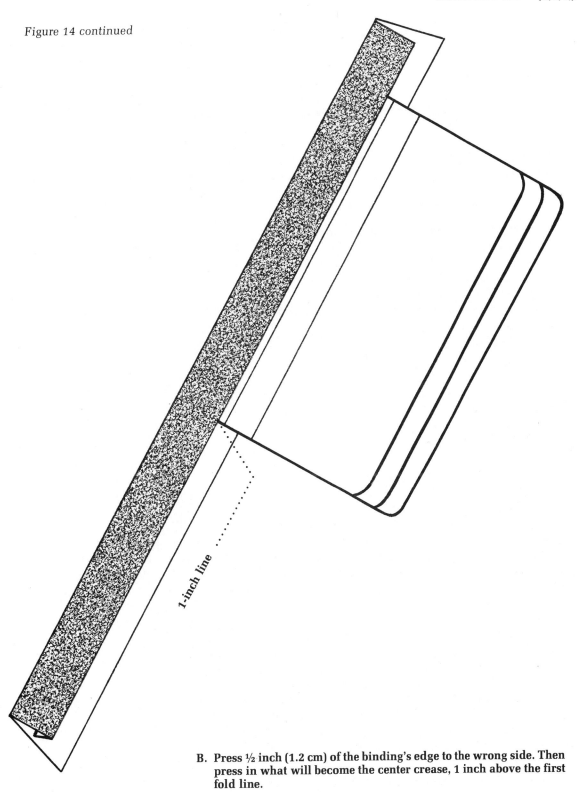

1-inch line ....

B. Press ½ inch (1.2 cm) of the binding's edge to the wrong side. Then press in what will become the center crease, 1 inch above the first fold line.

Baby's Butterfly Quilt (QQQQ)

Reverse appliqué traditionally involves hand-hemming, embroidery, and tedium. Here the same effect—a cut-away silhouette over a contrasting background—is achieved with 4-Q quickness.

To make this quilt you will need:

- 1⅓ yards of cotton fabric at least 45 inches wide
- 1⅓ yards of *double-faced* prequilted fabric at least 45 inches wide, in a contrasting color
- 5½ yards of blanket binding
- thread to match the cotton and the prequilted fabric
- fusible webbing (*not* interfacing)
- a sewing machine with a size 9 or 11 (European size 65 or 75) needle, a quilting guide attachment, a zigzag stitch, and a quilting foot
- an ironing board and an iron
- pattern paper with a 1-inch grid
- pattern weights
- a French curve
- a washable marker
- 30 large (1½-inch) safety pins (reusable)
- common pins
- fabric shears

Prewash and dry the fabrics.

Cut a 48 × 45-inch rectangle from the cotton. Cut a 48 × 45-inch rectangle from the prequilted fabric.

On the pattern paper, draft the butterfly to scale, or draw your own (Figure 15A). If you use the method of reverse appliqué that follows, you will not need to add seam allowances around the perimeter of the silhouette you draw. Use an *unthreaded* sewing machine and a stitch length of 12 (2.5 for metric machines) to sew over the paper butterfly's outline. Lay the pattern wrong side up over the wrong side of the cotton rectangle. Use pattern weights to hold the pattern in place. Trace repeatedly over the perforated outline of the butterfly with the washable marker. Draw a diagonal line from one corner to another on the right side of the cotton rectangle.

Thread the machine. Leave the stitch length at 12 (2.5 for metric machines). Lower the needle into the butterfly outline. With the stitch-length adjustment temporarily set on zero, take three to five stitches in place. Then stitch around the outline of the butterfly, but *not over the antennae*. To finish the line of stitching, take three to five stitches in place.

Trim the *inside* of the butterfly to within ½ inch of the stitched outline (what to do with the scraps?—save them to use in a quilt, of course). Clip the curves, being careful not to cut into stitching. Lay the cotton rectangle wrong side up on the ironing board. Fold the seam allowance to the inside on the seam line and press it. Place fusible webbing under the seam allowances and press again.

Now lay the cotton rectangle right side up over the prequilted rectangle. Secure the two layers together with well-distributed safety pins. Place common pins around the butterfly outline, perpendicular to the line of stitching. Loosen slightly the pressure on the presser foot.

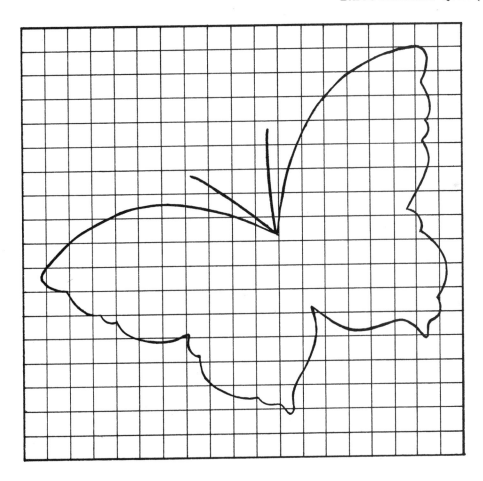

Figure 15. Baby's Butterfly Quilt.
A. Use this butterfly as a pattern (SCALE: one square equals 2 square inches), or draw your own butterfly, star, duckling, or other shape. You will not need to allow for seam allowances.

Using a straight stitch of 12 (2.5 for metric machines) and top and bobbin threads matching the cotton, topstitch over the outline of the butterfly, removing any pins in your path. Begin and end by taking three to five stitches in place. Draw the antennae with the washable marker. Use a stitch length of 20 (0.5 for metric machines), a narrow zigzag setting, top thread matching the pre-quilted material, and bobbin thread matching the cotton, to sew over the inked-on antennae.

For the quilt stitching, use a straight-stitch, a stitch length of 9 (3 for metric machines), slightly loosened presser-foot pressure, a quilting-guide attachment setting of 2 inches, top thread matching the cotton rectangle, and bobbin thread matching the prequilted fabric. Do the first row of quilt stitching by simply sewing over the washable ink line from the upper corner to the edge of the butterfly; resume again at the lower edge of the butterfly and follow the line out to the opposite corner. *Don't quilt over the butterfly.* Remove any safety pins in your path; *don't try to sew over safety pins.* Align the quilting guide with the row you've just sewn, and sew a second row 2 inches distant from and parallel to the first. Quilt subsequent rows by aligning the quilting-guide attachment with the last row quilted. Where you must, quilt-stitch further to the interior than the previous quilt-stitching line went (because it was interrupted earlier by the

Figure 15 continued

B. With the washable marker, make a diagonal line from one corner to the opposite corner. Quilt-stitch over it; then quilt-stitch in parallel rows 2 inches apart, stopping at the butterfly's perimeter. You may have to draw in more diagonal lines later, where the line to be quilted reaches farther into the interior of the quilt than the previous row of stitching.

butterfly's outline), use the washable marker to draw in the missing segment of the previous line (see Figure 15B). When you reach the corner of the quilt, turn the quilt around, align the quilting-guide attachment with the other side of the original diagonal line, and quilt to the opposite corner.

Press one end of the blanket binding under ½ inch. Encase the raw edges of the quilt in the blanket binding, beginning with the pressed end. Miter corners (see page 7), and pin. When you come to the pressed end, cut the other end of the blanket binding, leaving 2 inches for overlapping. Unpin the first pin, lay the unpressed end under the pressed end, and repin. Leave the presser-foot pressure slightly loosened, and set the stitch-length adjustment for 12 (2.5 for metric machines). Sew twice around the blanket binding, ¼ and ⅛ inch from the inside edge.

Follow the manufacturer's instructions to remove ink lines.

This quilt is fully machine-washable and -dryable on warm and gentle cycles. Do not line-dry or press this or any other quilt.

Border-Print Quilt (QQQ)

This design pursues an aesthetic goal of modern quilting: to have the quilt-stitching pattern and the pattern made by the color contrasts of the quilt top enhance each other. Old-fashioned quilters superimposed quilt-stitching designs—such as hearts—arbitrarily over unrelated patchwork patterns—such as squares—creating a "wiggle-picture" effect; sometimes one saw hearts, sometimes squares, but not both simultaneously. Here the two patterns are integrated.

And, of course, this design is quick. Two lengths of border-print fabric are simply sewn together along the non-border edges. The center details are added by a streamlined method of reverse appliqué.

You will need:

- 5 yards of border-print fabric at least 36 inches wide
- 5 square yards of 4-ounce *bonded* polyester batting
- 1 square yard of fabric that contrasts with the non-border part of the border-print fabric
- a full flat sheet for the quilt bottom
- 9½ yards of quilt binding
- thread matching the non-border part of the border-print fabric
- fusible webbing (*not* interfacing)
- a sewing machine with a size 9 or 11 (European size 65 or 75) needle, a 6-inch quilting guide attachment, and a quilting foot
- an ironing board and an iron
- a yardstick
- pattern paper with a 1-inch grid
- a French curve
- carbon paper
- pattern weights
- a washable ink marker
- 80 or so large (1½-inch) safety pins (reusable)
- common pins
- fabric shears

Prewash and dry the fabrics and the sheet. If the border print is wider than 36 inches, use the washable marker and the measuring stick to delineate the excess *along the non-border edge*; trim away the excess.

Fold the border-print fabric in half widthwise and pin; press in a crease. Cut on the crease. Pin the two halves together along the non-border selvage edges, right sides together. Use a stitch length of 16 (2 for metric machines) to sew a ¼-inch (0.6-cm) seam. Then press the seam allowances open.

Using a pencil and a French curve, draft the flower pattern onto pattern paper with a 1-inch grid (Figure 16A). Don't cut out the pattern piece; instead, use an unthreaded sewing machine to perforate the outline of the flower. Make the large stem piece by drawing two 18-inch-long lines at a right angle to each other on pattern paper. Mark a point 4½ inches above the intersection of the first two lines; use the yardstick to connect this point to the ends of the lines. Perforate the outline with an unthreaded sewing machine.

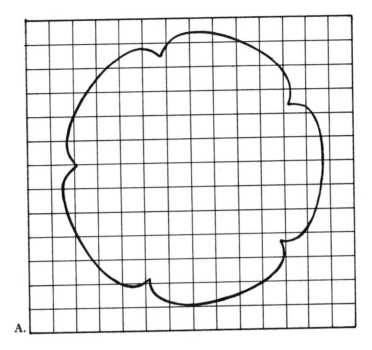

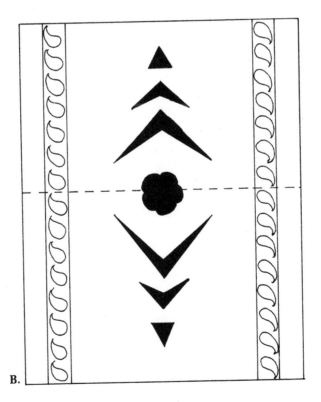

Figure 16. Border-Print Quilt.
A. The flower pattern. SCALE: each square equals 1 square inch.
B. Arrange the pattern pieces along the crease (the broken line) and the center seam.

Figure 16 continued

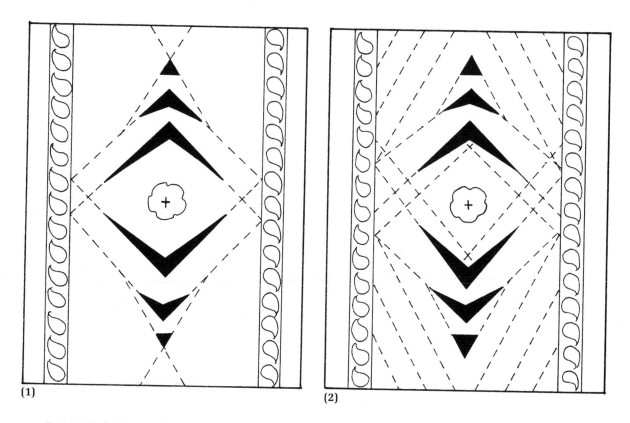

(1)   (2)

C. (1) Mark these quilting lines if the border is contained in a panel.
(2) Quilt-stitching lines for a border print contained in a panel.

For the second stem piece, the first two pairs of lines are 12 inches long and at right angles to each other. Mark the point 4½ inches above the intersection of these lines; connect the point to the ends of the first two lines.

For the little triangle piece, draft a 4½-inch square. Bisect the bottom side of the square. Connect the two top corners of the square with the center of the bottom line.

Perforate all the pattern pieces.

Fold the border fabric in half widthwise; press in a crease. Center the flower pattern piece over the intersection of the crease and the seam. Locate the stem pieces along the seam, with the center of the large stem piece 12 inches below the flower, the small stem piece 4½ inches below the large stem piece, and the triangle 4½ inches below the small stem piece (Figure 16B). Use pattern weights to hold the pieces in place. Trace repeatedly over the perforation lines with the washable marker to transfer the outlines onto the quilt. Then invert the stem and the triangle pieces and arrange them correspondingly above the flower; use a washable marker to trace their outlines through the perforations.

Sew over the inked-on outlines. Use a stitch length of 16 (2 for metric machines), but begin by setting the stitch-length adjustment temporarily on zero and taking three to five stitches in place. End each outline by stitching in place again.

Then trim away the fabric *inside* the outline of the flower, to within ½ inch of the seam line. Clip the curves, being careful not to cut into the seam. Fold the seam allowances to the inside of

Figure 16 continued

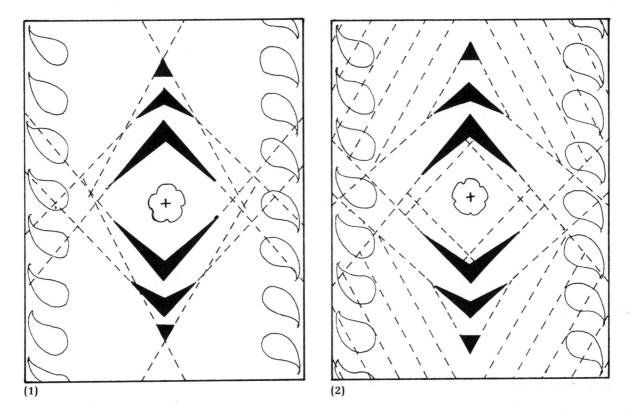

(1)   **(2)**

D. (1) **Mark these quilting lines if the border print has no panel.**
   (2) **Quilt-stitching lines for a border print having no panel.**

the seam line; press. Place strips of fusible webbing between the seam allowances and the wrong side of the fabric. Press again.

Cut a square of contrasting fabric slightly larger than the flower. Lay it right side up. Then lay the border-print fabric right side up over it, so that the contrasting fabric shows through the flower-shaped hole. Pin. With a stitch length of 16 (2 for metric machines), topstitch around the edges of the outline, beginning and ending by taking three to five stitches in place. On the wrong side of the fabric, trim the square of contrasting fabric *outside* the topstitching to make it even with the seam allowance of the border fabric. Press the contrasting fabric's seam allowance toward the border fabric. Lay strips of fusible webbing between the seam allowances and press again.

Trim away the fabric inside the other outlines *one at a time*; sew in pieces of contrasting fabric.

Then mark the quilting lines with a washable marker as shown in Figure 16C or 16D, depending on whether or not your border design includes a panel.

Lay the sheet (the quilt bottom) wrong side up on the floor and smooth out any wrinkles. Lay the quilt top over it, aligning a corner of the quilt top with a corner of the sheet. Pin the quilt top and the sheet together with a few safety pins at the corner and along the two adjoining edges. Smooth out the quilt top. Then trim away the excess sheet extending beyond the area of the quilt top. Set the quilt top aside. Lay batting over the quilt bottom. Cut and piece the batting to conform to the size of the quilt bottom. Lay the quilt top, right side up, over the batting. *Without lifting the quilt,* secure all three layers together with safety pins. Distribute the safety pins over the whole area of the quilt.

To do the quilt stitching, release the presser-foot pressure slightly and set the stitch-length adjustment for 9 (3 for metric machines). Lower the needle into the fabric through a quilt-stitching line. Place one hand below and the other hand above the quilt; smooth out wrinkles along the quilt-stitching line. With the stitch-length adjustment temporarily set on zero, take three to five stitches in place. Then do the quilt stitching, removing the safety pins from your path. *Don't try to sew over safety pins.* Begin and end each quilt-stitching line by stitching in place. Use the quilt-stitching guide at its maximum setting to quilt the lines parallel to the marked lines.

Encase the edges in quilt binding, mitering the corners (see page 7); pin with common pins. Sew two rows of topstitching, one ⅛ inch and one ¼ inch from the inside edges of the quilt binding. Or, use a twin needle and topstitch once.

Launder to remove washable ink lines, following the manufacturer's instructions. Do not line-dry or press this or any other quilt.

Six Moons of Saturn (Q)

Creating these extraterrestrial textures by conventional quilting methods would involve painstaking trapunto. However, a streamlined technique makes this quilt light-years quicker.

Before beginning, look at the color photograph of this quilt following page 50. To make this full-size bedspread and accompanying pillow shams, you will need:

- three identical full-size flat blue sheets
- one tan or off-white (*not* white) flat twin sheet for the foreground moon (Dione) and the ruffles
- fabric remnants for Saturn, the light shadow across Saturn, Saturn's rings, and the other moons (Naturalistic colors have been used, but you may want to make all the non-blue pieces—including Dione and the ruffles—the same contrasting color, such as silver; if so, omit the light shadow across Saturn)
- 9¼ square yards of *bonded* 5-ounce polyester batting
- ¾ yards of cording
- fusible *interfacing* for Saturn's rings
- thread to match the blue sheets, the other sheet, the rings, Saturn's light shadow, and Saturn
- a sewing machine with a zigzag stitch, a 6-inch quilting-guide attachment, a size 9 or 11 (European size 65 or 75) needle, and a quilting foot
- an ironing board and an iron
- pattern paper
- a French curve
- a large compass, or a pencil and a string
- pattern weights
- a washable marker
- approximately 60 large (1½-inch) safety pins (reusable)
- paper-cutting scissors
- fabric shears
- one very small safety pin
- common pins

Cut out the blue pieces, using the layout scheme shown in Figure 17A.

To make the pattern pieces for Dione (the big moon in the foreground), construct a circle with a radius of 9¼ inches. Cut one such circle from the remnants of the blue sheets and one from the batting. Then use the French curve to draw a line separating the light from the dark sections of the paper moon. Cut on the curved line. Place the two paper pattern pieces on paper; anchor them with pattern weights. Measure and mark points ½ inch from the inside edges. Connect the points. Draw and cut around the outside edges of the two moon pieces, and on the curved seam-allowance lines you've just made. Use the pattern pieces to cut the light (tan or off-white) and the dark (blue) sections of Dione. Pin these two sections right sides together along the seam allowance lines and sew—with a stitch length of 12 (2.5 for metric machines)—a ½-inch (1.2-cm) seam. Press the seam open; clip if necessary.

Use the washable marker to draw eight craters, ranging from 1¼ to 4¾ inches in diameter, on the light side of Dione. Position one of these craters so that it is half in shadow—that is, half on the blue side and half on the off-white side. One small crater should be inside the largest crater. Now lay the moon top over the bottom with right sides together. Pin; sew a ½-inch (1.2-cm) seam

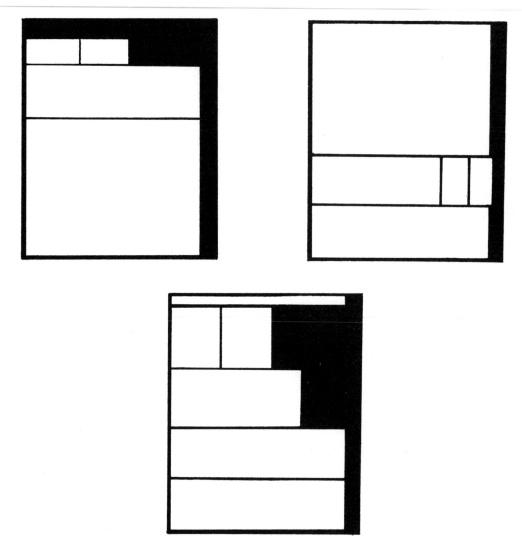

Figure 17.   Six Moons of Saturn.
A. **Cut the bedspread and the sham pieces from three blue full-size flat sheets.**

   TOP LEFT SHEET: **the quilt top's center piece (56 × 77 inches), one 22 × 77-inch side segment, and two corner flap pieces (each 12 × 22 inches).**

   TOP RIGHT SHEET: **one 22 × 77-inch side piece, one 22 × 56-inch end segment, two 12 × 22-inch corner flap pieces, and** most **of the quilt bottom's center piece (it will have to be pieced to another segment cut from the third sheet).**

   BOTTOM SHEET: **two 22 × 77-inch side pieces, one 22 × 56-inch end piece, two pillow sham top pieces (each 21 × 27 inches), and the remainder of the quilt bottom's center piece (the upper edge of the sheet). Save the leftover blue fabric to use as facings and shadows for the moons and Saturn.**

around the entire circumference. Clip the seam. In the *bottom (the all-blue)* piece, cut a slash; turn Dione right side out through it. Press Dione flat. Insert the batting through the slash and quickly slip-stitch the slash shut (neatness doesn't count). Secure all three layers together with safety pins.

   The craters are formed by quilting and cording. Loosen the pressure on the presser foot slightly and adjust the zigzag control to a very narrow position. Begin by setting the stitch-length

Figure 17 continued

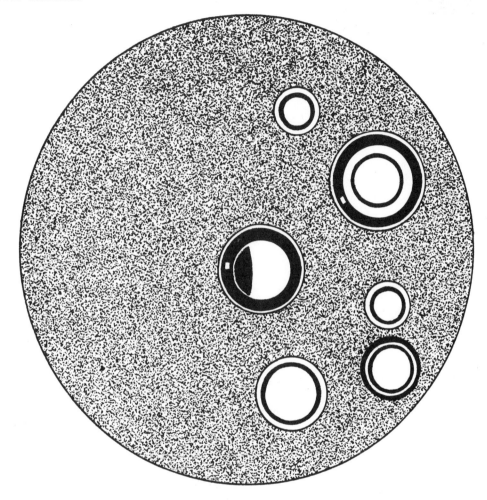

B. **The reverse side of Dione. The craters have been created by quilt-stitching over the washable ink circles and in concentric rings ¼ inch inside the ink circles. The quilting on the crater that is half in shadow has been done half in blue thread, half in off-white thread. The** *bottom* **(facing) fabric and the batting inside each crater's rim—that is, between the two concentric rings of quilt stitching—is left intact. Cording, pulled by a tiny safety pin through the channels between the two largest craters' concentric rings of quilt stitching, accentuates the rims of the craters.**

regulator temporarily on zero and taking three to five stitches in place. Place a hand above and a hand below the quilt to smooth out wrinkles. Using a stitch length of 12 (2.5 for metric machines), sew over the washable ink circles, removing any safety pins in your path. *Don't try to sew over safety pins.* Finish the circle by taking another three to five stitches in place. Then sew a concentric ring ¼ inch (0.6 cm) inside each inked crater rim. Begin and end every ring of quilting by stitching in place. When sewing the crater that is half in shadow, stop at the seam, take three to five stitches in place, change to blue thread, stitch in place, sew to the other seam, and stitch in place again.

On the *reverse* side of Dione (see Figure 17B), carefully trim away the bottom fabric and the batting inside each crater. Leave the batting and the bottom fabric between the concentric rings on the craters' rims. In the largest crater, which has a small crater inside it, trim away the bottom

Figure 17 continued

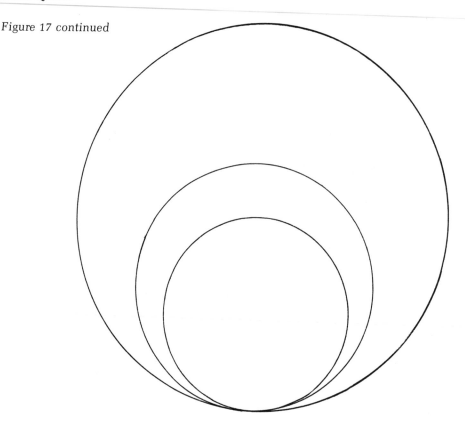

C. The moon patterns. Cut two of the smallest circle, and one of each of the others.

fabric and the batting between the rim of the outside crater and the rim of the inside crater; trim also inside the inside crater, leaving intact the batting and the bottom fabric inside the small crater's rim. Make a careful snip in the ¼-inch-wide bottom fabric between the outside concentric rings. Attach a very small safety pin to an end of the cording and push the pin through the ¼-inch-wide channel. When the pin has pulled the cording around the whole circumference, detach the pin, cut away the excess cording, attach the pin to the unused cording, and thread the cording through the rim of another large crater.

Make each of the four smaller moons (Encelcus, Rhea, Titan, Mimas, and Tethys; not all of Saturn's moons are visible from this perspective) by cutting a whole circle from the blue sheet remnants (for the bottom), a contrasting fabric remnant (for the top), and batting (Figure 17C). Then cut the shadow pieces from the blue remnants (Figure 17D) and press the inside edges under ½ inch (1.2 cm). Lay each shadow-piece right side up over the right side of the top (the non-blue) circle; pin. With the presser-foot pressure on normal setting and the stitch-length adjustment set for 12 (2.5 for metric machines), topstitch over the pressed edge of the shadow as close to the edge as possible. Then pin the bottom circle to the top, right sides together, and sew, using a ½-inch (1.2-cm) seam. Clip the seam, slash the *bottom* piece, and turn the moon right side out through the slash. Press the moon flat and insert the circle of batting. Hand-baste the slash closed if necessary.

To make the Saturn pattern, draw a paper circle 10 inches in diameter. Use it to cut batting, the bottom (blue) piece, and the top piece (from a contrasting color). From the blue sheet remnants cut two of the shadow pieces also (Figure 17E). Cut the light shadow from another color. Press under ½ inch (1.2 cm) of the inward-facing edges of the two curved shadow pieces. Press

Figure 17 continued

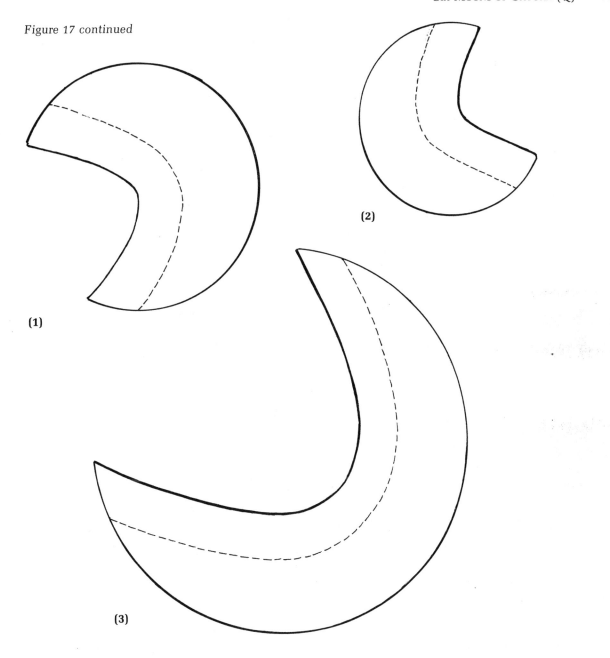

(2)

(1)

(3)

D. Cut the moon *shadows* **from** *blue* **(background) fabric. Press under the inside edges along the dash lines, clipping the curves as necessary.**

under the two long edges of the two rectangular shadows ½ inch (1.2 cm). Fold the Saturn top piece in half and press in a crease. Position the blue shadow right side up over the right side of the Saturn top piece so that the shadow's top corners touch the crease; pin. Lay the light shadow right side up on Saturn's top piece, parallel to and 1½ inches above the blue shadow; pin. Topstitch over the pressed edges of the shadows with a stitch length of 12 (2.5 for metric

Figure 17 continued

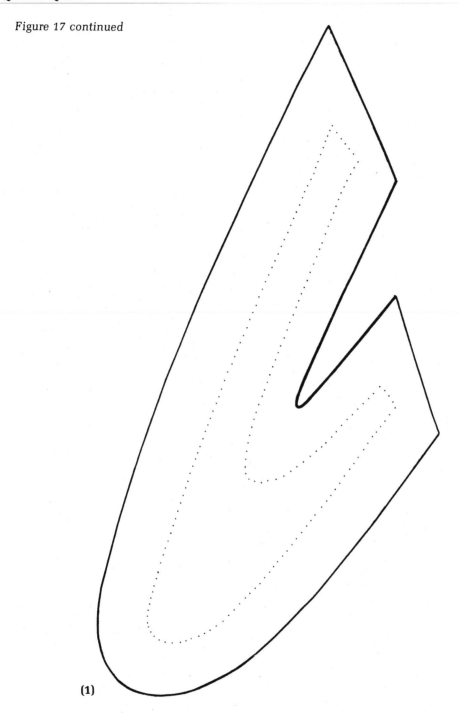

(1)

E. Rings. Cut fabric on the outside lines, interfacing on the dotted lines.
   (1) Saturn's right inner ring.

machines). Then position the smaller of the two curved shadows over the right edge of the Saturn top piece so that the crease bisects the curved shadow; pin. Place the larger curved shadow over the top edge of the Saturn piece so that the right corner of the shadow just touches the upper edge

Figure 17E. continued

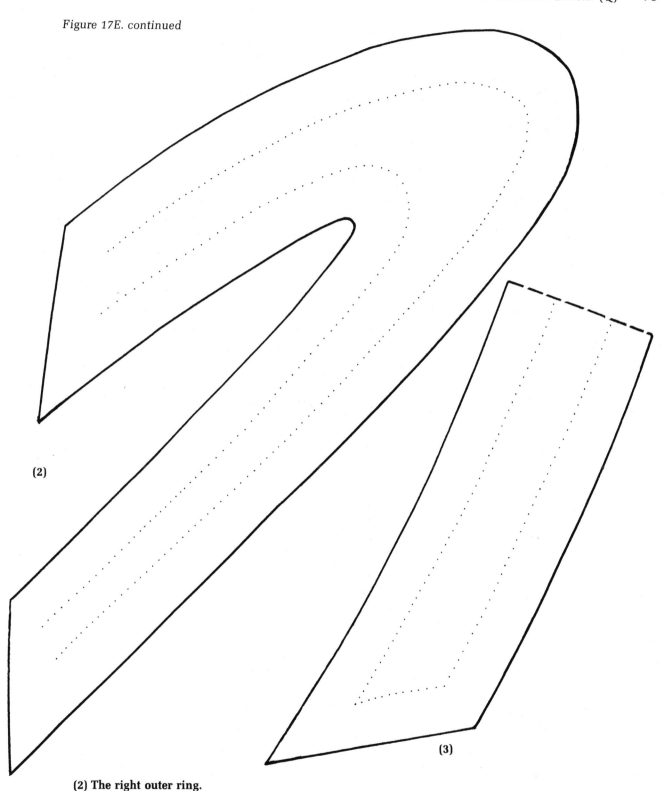

(2)

(3)

(2) The right outer ring.
(3) The blue (background fabric) shadow on Saturn. Place the edge with the broken line on the fold
 of the fabric before cutting.

Figure 17E. continued

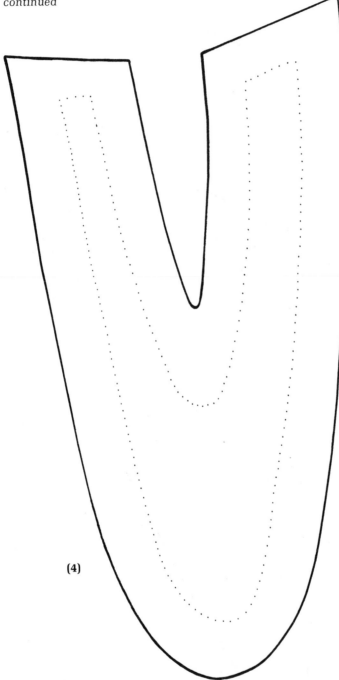

(4)

(4) Saturn's left inner ring.

Figure 17E. continued

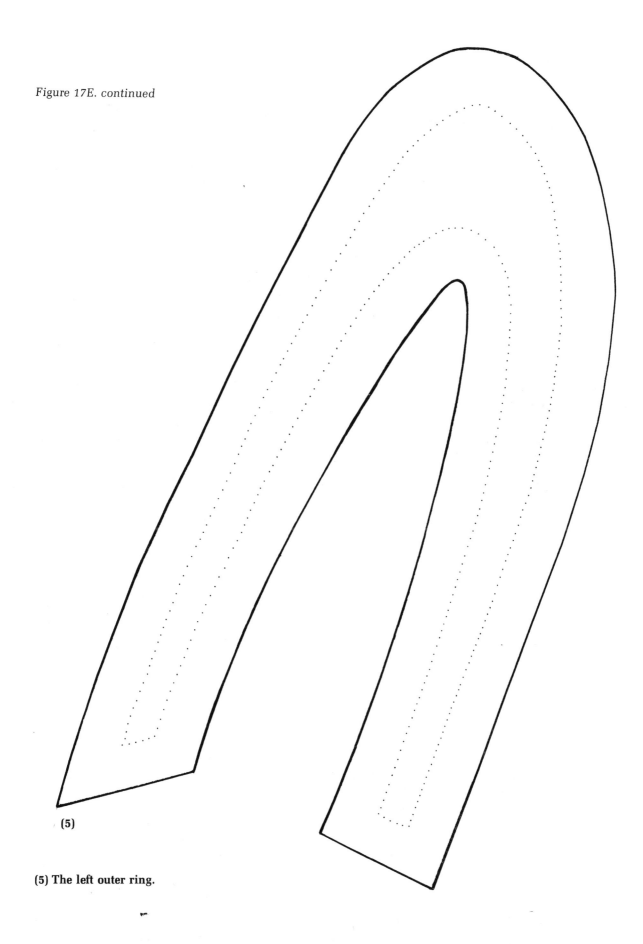

(5)

(5) The left outer ring.

Figure 17E. continued

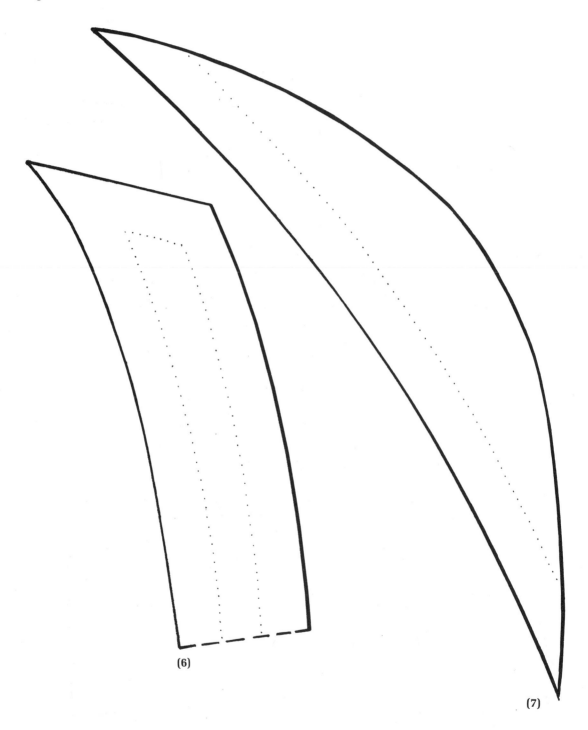

(6) The ring segment that passes in front of Saturn. Place the edge with the broken line on the fold of
    the fabric when cutting.
(7) The blue (background fabric) shadow on Saturn's right side.

Figure 17E. continued

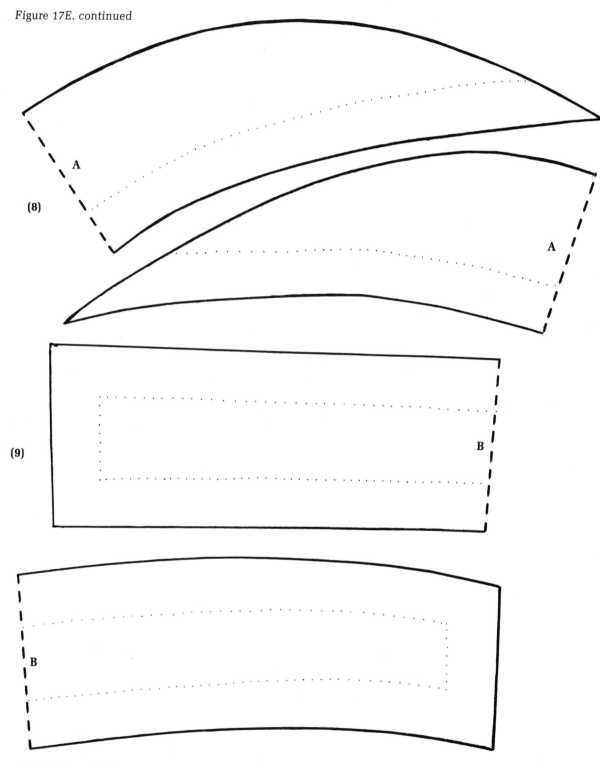

(8) The blue shadow on Saturn's upper edge. Join the pattern pieces exactly at the dotted line to make a whole pattern piece *before* cutting fabric or interfacing. Press the raw edges of these curved blue shadows under on the dotted lines before topstitching them onto Saturn.

(9) Saturn's light (non-blue) shadow. Join pattern pieces as described for (8) before cutting.

of the smaller curved shadow; pin. Topstitch over the pressed edges of the curved shadows. Pin the top Saturn piece to the bottom Saturn piece with right sides together. Sew a ½-inch (1.2-cm) seam around the entire circumference. Clip the seam. In the *bottom* Saturn piece cut a slash and turn Saturn right side out through it. Press Saturn flat. Insert the batting through the slash. Hand-baste the slash closed.

To make Saturn's rings, use the outside lines of the pattern (Figure 17E) to cut the fabric; use the inside lines to cut the fusible interfacing. The interfacing is the size the finished rings will be. Center the interfacing over the wrong sides of the ring fabric; press according to the interfacing manufacturer's instructions. After the interfacing has cooled, clip the curves in the fabric extending beyond the edges of the interfacing and fold the fabric back over the edges of the interfacing; press. Trim away any excess fabric that shows. For the "straight" ring segment, trim sparingly and use a strip of interfacing to hold down the raw edges. With a stitch length of 12 (2.5 for metric machines), topstitch along the two long edges of the "straight" ring segment. Then position the "straight" ring segment over the ends of the other ring segments, right sides together. Sew a ½-inch (1.2-cm) seam. Press the seam allowances toward the "straight" ring segment; topstitch over the seams; trim the seam allowances.

With right sides together, pin the two segments of the center quilt-bottom piece. Sew, using a stitch length of 9 (3 for metric machines). Its finished size should be exactly 77 × 56 inches. Press the seam allowances open.

Using Figure 17F as a guide, lay Dione, the other moons, Saturn, and the rings on the top center background blue piece. Note that the left ends of both rings go beneath Saturn, and the upper edge of Dione overlaps Saturn. Draw around each piece with a washable marker. Then draw an oval connecting Saturn's topmost and bottommost points with points ¾ inch to the left and the right of the outermost reaches of the rings (Figure 17G).

Place the top and bottom center blue rectangles right sides together and pin the upper edge. Set the stitch-length adjustment for 9 (3 for metric machines) and sew a ½-inch (1.2-cm) seam. Press the seam allowances open. Then fold the seam closed—with right sides of the fabric out—and press the seam flat. Lay the center rectangle bottom wrong side up on the floor, opening out the top. Smooth out wrinkles. Cut a piece of batting to the dimensions of the center rectangle. The batting should touch the seam at the upper edge and the raw edges on the other three edges. Lay the batting over the bottom piece. Fold the top piece over the batting. Smooth out wrinkles. *Without lifting the quilt,* use large safety pins to secure all three layers together.

To do the quilt stitching, loosen the pressure on the presser foot slightly and leave the stitch length at 9 (3 for metric machines). Place a hand above and a hand below the quilt to smooth out wrinkles. Lower the needle into the washable ink oval, set the stitch-length adjustment temporarily on zero, and take three to five stitches in place. Quilt-stitch over the outline of the oval. Remove safety pins as you come to them. *Don't try to sew over safety pins.* When the oval is completed, take another three to five stitches in place and cut the thread. Set the quilting-guide attachment for 3 inches—or use a small quilting guide at its maximum setting—and sew the second row of quilt stitching as a larger oval parallel to the first. Subsequent rows of quilting are in concentric ovals. Remember periodically to place hands above and beneath the quilt to smooth out wrinkles, and to begin and end each oval by taking three to five stitches in place. Quilt to the four corners of the rectangle.

Pin the rings and all the moons except Dione in place. Release the presser-foot pressure slightly more and set the stitch-length adjustment for 12 (2.5 for metric machines). Topstitch around the edges of the moons, using blue thread to sew over the shadow sections; use top thread matching the non-blue sections when you sew over them. Use blue bobbin thread throughout.

Figure 17 continued

F. After making Saturn and the moons, arrange them on the quilt top's center (56 × 77-inch) piece. Draw around them with the washable marker.

Topstitch over the outside edges of the rings, but *not* over the center ring segment. Pin and topstitch Saturn, and then Dione, in place.

Place the two end pieces (the 56 × 22-inch rectangles) right sides together. Pin them along the 22-inch-long edges. With the presser-foot pressure on a normal setting, sew a ½-inch (1.2-cm) seam at each end. Press the seam allowance open. Then fold the seams closed and press them flat. Turn the end pieces wrong sides out and press to the inside the bottom ½ inch. Cut a piece of batting to the size of the end piece, and position it so that it touches the side seams, the bottom fold, and the raw edges at the top. Pin the right sides of the unpressed edges of the end piece to the center piece by turning the end piece wrong side out and sliding it over the end of the center

Figure 17 continued

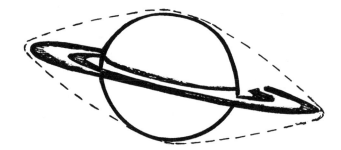

G. Draw an oval connecting these four points: Saturn's upper edge, Saturn's lower edge, and the outermost reaches (left and right) of the outside rings. This oval is the first line of quilt stitching. Subsequent quilting lines are concentric ovals 3 inches apart. Quilt to the outside of the center piece; then topstitch the moons and Saturn around their circumferences.

piece. Lay the batting over the end piece, remove the pins one at a time, and replace them through the batting as well as the center and the end pieces. Release the pressure on the presser foot slightly and sew a ½-inch (1.2-cm) seam. Trim away the *batting's* seam allowance. Turn the end piece right side out over the batting; use common pins to secure the pressed edges together. Then, with the presser-foot pressure on a nearly normal setting, topstitch twice over the outside edge of the end piece's pressed edges.

To quilt-stitch the end piece, lay the quilt flat on the floor, smooth out wrinkles in the end section, and secure all of the layers of the end section together with large safety pins. Set the 6-inch quilting guide attachment at its maximum setting, loosen the presser-foot pressure slightly, and set the stitch-length adjustment for 9 (3 for metric machines). Begin at the upper right edge of the piece so that the machine does not have to accommodate the bulk of the quilt. Align the quilting guide with the next-to-the-last row of quilt stitching on the center piece. After taking three to five stitches in place, follow that row until the quilting guide meets the top edge of the end piece; then quilt a straight line parallel to the seam until the quilting guide meets the intersection of the center piece's next-to-the-last row of quilting (on the left side) and the seam. Follow the next-to-the-last row of quilt stitching to the left edge of the end piece. At the end, take three to five stitches in place; clip threads. Sew the second row of quilt stitching parallel to the first.

Attach the two side pieces by sewing the end seams of the two pairs of 22 × 77-inch rectangles, pressing the outer edges under ½ inch, cutting batting to fit, and sewing the batting and the right sides of the side pieces to the sides of the center piece. Then trim away the seam allowance of the batting, turn the side pieces right side out, and topstitch twice over the outer (pressed) edges. Distribute safety pins.

Quilt-stitch the side pieces by aligning the 6-inch quilting-guide attachment—at its maximum setting—with the next-to-the-last row of the center piece's quilt stitching; follow that row until the quilting guide meets the edge of the side piece; then quilt a straight line until the quilting guide meets the intersection with the next-to-the-last row of the center piece's quilt stitching. Finally, follow this row of quilt stitching to the edge of the side piece. Quilt-stitch a second row parallel to the first. See Figure 17H.

To make the two corner flaps, use one of the corner flap pieces to cut two such pieces from batting. Place two blue fabric pieces right sides together; pin. Lay them over a piece of batting. Remove the pins one at a time; repin. With the presser-foot pressure slightly loosened, sew a ½-inch (1.2-cm) seam around the sides, the bottom, and 1 inch on each side of the top edges;

Figure 17 continued

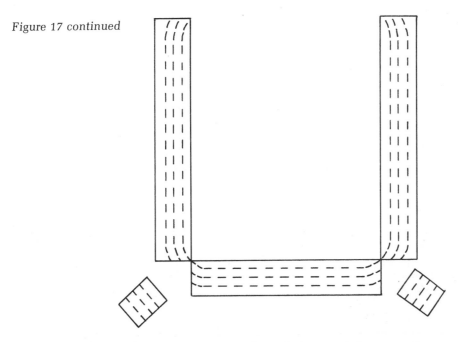

H. Quilt-stitching lines on the side pieces, the end piece, and the corner flaps.

leave the rest of the top open. Trim the batting seam allowance. Clip the fabric at the corners. Turn the flaps right sides out. Fold the top edges in ½ inch (1.2 cm), and topstitch over the top edges. Then, with a stitch-length setting of 9 (3 for metric machines), quilt-stitch in rows parallel to and 6 inches away from the top edge of each flap.

To attach the flaps to the quilt, center the flaps over the lower corners of the center piece *on the inside*. Pin the flaps to the upper edges of the end and side pieces and slip-stitch by hand along the top edges.

Laundering the quilt on warm and gentle cycles (or according to the manufacturer's instruction) will remove the washable ink lines. Dry the quilt alternately on permanent press and fluff settings. Because of the quilt's bulk, for best results use commercial machines.

The Pillow Shams (QQ)

Use one of the 27 × 21-inch blue sham pieces as a pattern to cut two more such rectangles from the Dione (the tan or off-white sheet) fabric, and two from the batting. With a washable marker, mark points at the outside lower corners and midway up the edges of the blue fabric that will eventually be in the center—that is, where the shams will meet; connect the marks with an arc (see Figure 18). Lay the batting pieces over the *wrong* side of the blue pieces and the Dione rectangles over the batting pieces. Safety-pin the three layers together. Loosen the presser-foot pressure slightly on the sewing machine, set the stitch-length adjustment for 9 (3 for metric machines), and quilt-stitch over the arcs. Begin and end every arc by taking three to five stitches in place with the stitch-length regulator temporarily on zero. Remove safety pins as you come to them. *Don't try to sew over safety pins.* Set the quilting-guide attachment for 3 inches and sew parallel rows of quilt stitching above and below the first arcs.

To make the ruffles, cut four 6-inch-wide strips the length of the sheet from which Dione was cut. With right sides together and the presser-foot pressure on a normal setting, sew the ends of one strip to the ends of another; repeat for the remaining pair of strips. Press the seam allowances open. Then fold each loop in half lengthwise, right sides out, and press. To divide each ruffle in quarters, align the two seams with each other, fold the ruffle flat, and mark the folds and the seams with a washable marker; these marks are the quarter divisions. With the stitch-length adjustment set at 6 (4 for metric machines), sew two rows of gathering stitches ¼ inch (0.6 cm) and ⅜ inch (0.9 cm) away from the raw edges of the ruffles, through both layers. Don't clip the ends of the gathering threads.

Pin the ruffles to the right sides of the blue pillow-sham fronts, matching the ruffles' quarter divisions to the midway points of each edge of the pillow-sham fronts. The folded edges of the ruffles should face inward. Gather the ruffles by carefully pulling the gathering threads. Use a stitch length of 6 (4 for metric machines) and a slightly loosened presser-foot pressure setting to baste the ruffles to the fronts, using a ½-inch (1.2-cm) seam.

Fold back a short edge of the sham pattern piece 9.5 inches so that the pattern now measures 21 × 17.5 inches. Cut four pieces of Dione fabric this size; finish one 21-inch edge of each by turning the raw edge under ¼ inch and sewing over it with a stitch length of 9 (3 for metric machines), then turning the edge under again and stitching over it once more, using a stitch-length setting of 9 (3 for metric machines). These pieces are the pillow-sham backs.

Lay the pillow-sham backs over the fronts, with right sides together. The backs will overlap each other about 4 inches in the center. Pin. Permanently sew the backs, the fronts, and the ruffles together with a stitch length of 12 (2.5 for metric machines) and a ½-inch-wide seam.

Cosmic dreams!

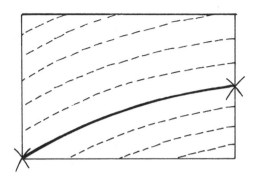 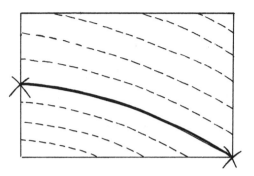

Figure 18.   Shams for Six Moons of Saturn.
Use a washable marker to draw the quilt-stitching lines on the pillow sham fronts. Connect points at the outside lower corners and midway in the center edge with an arc. Subsequent rows of quilt stitching run parallel to, and 3 inches away from, the marked arcs.

Quilt Slip (QQQQ)

Zip the quilt slip around its ample comforter, spread the comforter over a bottom sheet, and you'll never have to make the bed again. Or use the comforter conventionally over two sheets and a light blanket. The comforter's case, or "quilt slip," zips off for easy washing.

To make a *double-bed* quilt slip (for other bed sizes, see "Quilt Slip Variations," page 91), you will need:

- two identical full flat sheets (HINTS: try to select sheets that don't look like sheets, avoiding those with white backgrounds, for example. Buy matching or coordinating pillow cases or pillow shams at the same time.)
- 32 inches of ½-inch-wide white twill tape
- two 36-inch zippers
- 2¼ yards of 3- or 4-inch-wide eyelet or other trim (optional)
- thread
- a sewing machine with a size 9 or 11 (European size 65 or 75) needle and a zipper foot
- an ironing board and an iron
- a yardstick
- common pins
- a washable marker
- fabric shears
- a seam ripper

Leave the top hem in *one* sheet, but remove the other hems. Prewash and dry the sheets by machine.

Cut 2 inches from the unhemmed end of the hemmed sheet. With right sides together, pin the 2-inch strip to the top end of the other sheet. Lay the zippers along the pinned edge, with their tabs nearly touching each other in the middle, and center the zippers along the edge. Mark the locations of the outside ends of the zippers with a washable marker. Set the zippers aside. Sew a ⅝-inch (1.5-cm) seam up to the first mark, with the presser-foot pressure on a normal setting and the stitch-length adjustment set for 12 (2.5 for metric machines). Set the stitch-length regulator temporarily on zero and take three to five stitches in place. Then machine-baste to the second mark with a stitch length of 6 (4 for metric machines); stitch in place again and permanently stitch to the end of the seam. Press the seam allowances open.

Lay the zippers right sides down along the seam and pin them in place. With a zipper foot and a stitch length of 6 (4 for metric machines), baste the zippers in place. From the outside, use the seam ripper to remove the basted segment of the ⅝-inch (1.5-cm) seam, exposing the zippers. Adjust the zippers if necessary. If the zippers need no correction, permanently stitch the zippers in place with a stitch-length setting of 12 (2.5 for metric machines).

With right sides together, pin and sew the bottom edges of the two sheets together, using a ½-inch (1.2-cm) seam and a stitch length of 9 (3 for metric machines). Press the seam allowances open.

Measure and mark points 89 inches below the upper edge of the sheet with the zippers in it. Connect the points—with a washable marker and a yardstick—to form a line. Fold the sheet on this line, wrong sides together, and press in a crease. Lay the sheets flat on the floor, folded on

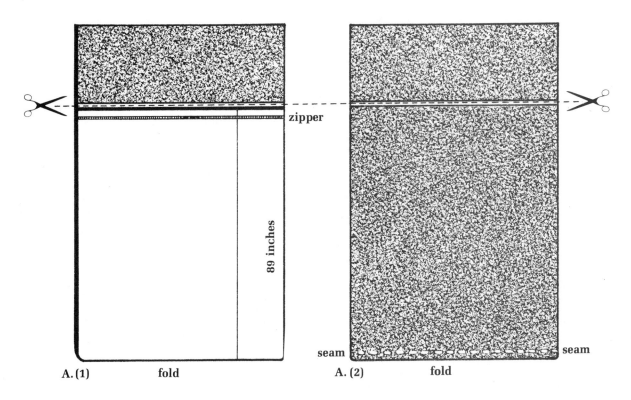

zipper

89 inches

A. (1)   fold

seam   seam

A. (2)   fold

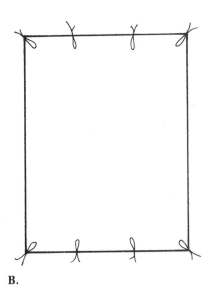

B.

Figure 19.   Quilt slip.
A. Measure and mark points on the longer (the hemmed) sheet 1 inch above the edge of the shorter (the zippered) sheet. (1) quilt slip top; (2) the quilt slip bottom.
B. Pin the sheets together with right sides together. Form equal lengths of twill tape into loops. Position them, with the loops facing inward, over the corners of the sheets and at ⅓ and ⅔ divisions along the upper and lower edges.

this line. Measure and mark points on the longer (the hemmed) sheet 1 inch above the edge of the shorter (the zippered) sheet. (See Figure 19A.) Connect the points with the measuring stick and the washable marker; cut on the line.

If you are adding the trim, lay the upper edge of the trim wrong side up over the wrong side of the hemmed edge of the segment you've just severed, so that the trim hangs downward from the hemmed edge; pin. Topstitch, with a stitch-length adjustment of 12 (2.5 for metric machines).

Fold under ½ inch (1.2 cm) along both *sides* of the hemmed segment; press.

Lay the hemmed segment right side up; lay the front (the zippered) sheet over it, with wrong side up; pin. Fold the two sheets together with right sides facing each other. Remove the pins one at a time and replace them through all three layers. Now pin the sides of the top sheet to the sides of the bottom sheet. Cut the twill tape into eight equal lengths, each four inches long. Form the tapes into loops and pin a loop over each corner of the sheets, with the loop facing the center of the quilt slip. Position the remaining loops along the upper and lower edges (Figure 19B). Using a stitch length of 9 (3 for metric machines), sew a ½-inch (1.2-cm) seam around the three edges. Double-stitch the corners to reinforce the loops. Clip the seam allowances at the corners.

Turn the quilt slip right side out through the zipper opening. Place pins around the perimeter of the quilt slip to hold the seams exactly at the outside edges, and press along the seams.

Set the stitch-length adjustment at 12 (2.5 for metric machines). Topstitch around all four edges, with a ¼-inch (0.6-cm) seam.

NOTE: On the upper edge, you will be pinning and topstitching through the upper edge of the hemmed segment.

Now slip in the comforter (see "Comforter," following), tie it in place with the twill tapes, and zip the quilt slip closed. Launder the quilt slip on warm and gentle cycles (remove the washable ink according to the manufacturer's instructions first, if necessary). You can make several of these quilt slips in different colors and alternate them.

Comforter (QQQ)

To make the comforter that goes inside the *double bed* quilt slip (for other bed sizes, see "Quilt Slips' Variations" on page 91), you will need:

- two *white* flat double-bed sheets
- 5¾ square yards of eight- or ten-ounce, *bonded* polyester batting
- 4 yards of ½-inch-wide white twill tape
- white thread
- heavy white crochet thread
- a sewing machine with a size 9 or 11 (European size 65 or 75) needle
- an ironing board and an iron
- a ruler or a Bishop hem guide (Dritz® Ezy-Hem® Guide)
- approximately 100 large (1½-inch) safety pins (reusable)
- common pins
- a needle with a large eye
- a needle threader
- fabric shears

Do not remove the hems from the sheets. Prewash and dry them by machine.

Shorten one sheet to 89 inches in length. Cut the twill tape into eight 18-inch lengths, fold

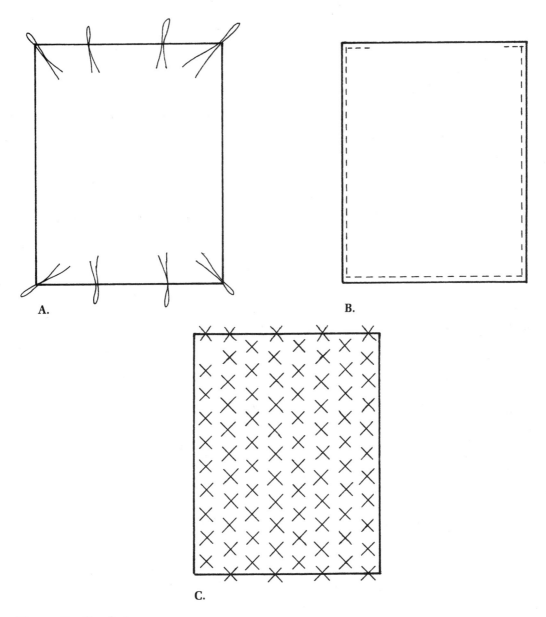

Figure 20.   Comforter.
A. **Cut the twill tape into eight 18-inch lengths. Fold them in half, and pin a tape over each corner on the** *right* **side of the shortened sheet and at ⅓ and ⅔ divisions along the upper and lower edges. Knot the ends of the twill tapes.**
B. **Sew around three edges, and the first inch and the last inch of the fourth edge. Then turn the comforter right side out.**
C. **Tie the quilt at 5-inch intervals in columns 5 inches apart, beginning alternate columns 0 and 2½ inches from the end.**

them in half and pin a tape over each corner and at ⅓ and ⅔ divisions along the upper and lower edges on the *right* side of the shortened sheet (as shown in Figure 20A). Knot the twill tape ends to prevent raveling.

Lay the second sheet over the first, right sides together; pin. Shorten the second sheet to

Figure 20 continued

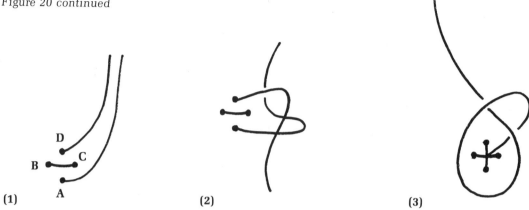

(1)   (2)   (3)

D. (1) **Insert the needle at Point A, and pull all but 2½ inches of the thread through to the bottom side of the comforter. Bring the needle back to the top side through Point B, reinsert it again at C, and bring it out again at D. Point A is ³/₁₆ inch from D; B is ³/₁₆ inch from C. Cut the longer end of the thread equal to the first.**

(2) **Tie the two thread ends in a simple knot—the first step of shoelace-tying.**

(3) **Then tie this knot, treating the two thread ends as a single thread. To finish, clip the thread ends to about ¾ inch.**

match the first. Lay the batting over the sheets; cut and piece sections of it together so that it conforms to the dimensions of the sheets. Remove the pins one at a time and replace them through all three layers.

Loosen the pressure on the presser foot slightly. With a stitch length of 9 (3 for metric machines) and the batting facing downward, sew a ½-inch (1.2-cm) seam around three edges, and the first inch and the last inch of the fourth edge (see Figure 20B). Double-stitch the seam over the ties to reinforce them. Turn the comforter right side out through the opening. Turn the raw edges in ½ inch at the opening; press. Trim the batting ½ inch at the opening. Pin the pressed edges together; topstitch the opening closed with a stitch length of 12 (2.5 for metric machines).

Lay the comforter flat on the floor and smooth out any wrinkles. *Without lifting it*, secure all three layers together with well-spaced safety pins.

To tie the comforter, first use a needle threader to pull about 4 inches of heavy crochet thread through the eye of the needle. Cut the other end of the thread about 40 inches long; don't knot the end.

Locate the knots as shown in Figure 20C: at 5-inch intervals in columns 5 inches apart, beginning alternate columns 0 and 2½ inches from the end.

To make a knot, insert the needle at Point **A**, as shown in Figure 20D. Pull all but 2½ inches of thread through to the bottom side of the comforter. Bring the needle back to the top side of the comforter through Point **B**; reinsert it at Point **C**; and bring it back up through Point **D**. Sever the longer end of the thread so that it too is 2½ inches long. Tie a simple knot, as shown in the illustration, and then tie the second knot shown. Clip both thread ends to about ¾ inch.

After making all the knots, remove the safety pins.

This polyester-filled comforter is easily machine-washable and dryable on warm and gentle cycles (for best results, use large commercial machines). However, the quilt slips, which zip on and off the comforter, prolong the life of the comforter by sparing it from frequent laundering. The slips are so easy to make that you can sew several and use them in rotation.

Quilt Slips Variations (QQQQ)

For a *twin* bed, buy *twin* (*not* full) size sheets for the comforter and the quilt slip, *one* (not two) 40-inch zipper, only 2 yards of the optional trim, and 4½ square yards of *bonded* batting. Follow the directions given for constructing the double-bed quilt slip and comforter.

For an *extra-long full* or an *extra-long twin* size, buy extra-long full (or extra-long twin) sheets, shorten the comforter's white sheets to 94 (instead of 89) inches, and measure 94 (instead of 89) inches from the upper edge of the quilt slip's top (zippered) sheet. You will need 6⅜ square yards of *bonded* batting for an extra-long full, 4⅞ square yards for an extra-long twin.

For a *queen-size* bed, buy *queen* (*not* full) size sheets for the comforter and the quilt slip. Shorten the comforter's white sheets to 94 (instead of 89) inches, and use 7 square yards of *bonded* batting. For the queen-size quilt slip, purchase one 84-inch (sleeping-bag length) zipper and 2½ yards of trim (optional). Measure 94 (instead of 89) inches from the upper edge of the top (the zippered) sheet in the queen-size quilt slip.

For a *king-size* (78 × 80 inches) bed, buy *king* (*not* full) size sheets for the comforter and the quilt slip. Shorten the white sheets to 94 (instead of 89) inches. Use 8¼ square yards of *bonded* batting. Also buy one 84-inch (sleeping-bag length) zipper and 3 yards of trim (optional). For the king quilt slip, measure 94 (instead of 89) inches from the upper edge of the top (the zippered) sheet.

For a *California king-size* bed (72 × 84 inches), buy *king* or *California* king-size sheets for the comforter and the quilt slip. Shorten the comforter's white sheets to 98 (instead of 89) inches. Use 8¼ square yards of *bonded* batting. Also buy one 84-inch (sleeping-bag length) zipper, 3 yards of trim (optional), and 1 yard of fabric at least 52 inches wide.

After preshrinking the fabric, cut it into two 46 × 18-inch pieces. Sew their ends together with right sides facing each other. Finish both short ends and put a 4-inch hem in one long edge. Use this fabric in place of the "hemmed segment" at the upper edge of the quilt slip, and sew the trim to it if desired.

For the California king quilt slip, measure 98 (instead of 89) inches from the upper edge of the top (the zippered) sheet.

A Bunting/Quilt (QQQQ)

Not only is this snug bunting reversible, but it unzips to lie flat. The quilt-stitching lines simply trace some of the lines of the plaid. To make it, you will need:

- plaid (or check or other design based on squares or rectangles) flannel at least 40½ inches square *after preshrinking*
- flannel in an all-over print, at least 40½ inches square *after preshrinking*
- a 40½-inch square of 4-ounce *bonded* polyester batting
- a 38-inch separating zipper
- thread
- a sewing machine with a size 9 or 11 (European size 65 or 75) needle and zipper and quilting feet
- a Bishop hem guide (Dritz® Ezy-Hem® Guide)
- an ironing board and an iron
- a yardstick
- about 45 large (1½-inch) safety pins (reusable)
- common pins
- fabric shears

Prewash and dry the flannels by machine.

Trim one piece of flannel to exactly 40½ inches square. Lay the batting over the *wrong* side of this flannel square. The batting may overlap the flannel; don't bother to trim it exactly now. Pin the batting and the flannel together along all four edges. Loosen the pressure on the presser foot very slightly. Baste ¼ inch (0.6 cm) from the edge around the entire perimeter, with the batting facing downward, using a stitch length of 6 (4 for metric machines). Then trim the *batting* close to the basting.

Lay the batted square on a flat surface, with the batted side facing downward. Lay the other piece of flannel over the square, wrong side up. Beginning at a corner, pin the two flannel pieces together with common pins along two adjoining edges. Sew the two pinned edges, with the batting facing downward, using a ¼-inch (0.6-cm) seam, a stitch-length setting of 12 (2.5 for metric machines), and the presser-foot pressure very slightly loosened.

Turn the square right side out. Press the sewn edges flat. Trim the unbatted flannel piece even with the two unsewn edges of the batted square. Use the Bishop hem guide to press under ¼ inch (0.6 cm) on the two unsewn edges.

Study the plaid flannel and think of a quilt-stitching scheme. This involves simply deciding which of the plaid's lines to use as guides for the quilt stitching. Plan to leave unquilted the area within 1 inch of the edges. Figure 21A suggests one simple pattern.

Lay the quilt on a flat surface and smooth out any wrinkles. Secure all three layers together with well-spaced safety pins *without lifting the quilt.*

To do the machine quilt stitching, leave the presser-foot pressure very slightly loosened, and use a stitch length of 9 (3 for metric machines). Begin by lowering the needle into one of the lines of the plaid that is to be quilted. Place one hand above and the other hand below the quilt to smooth out wrinkles. Lower the presser foot and, with the stitch-length regulator temporarily set on zero, sew three to five stitches in place. Then quilt-stitch according to your scheme, removing

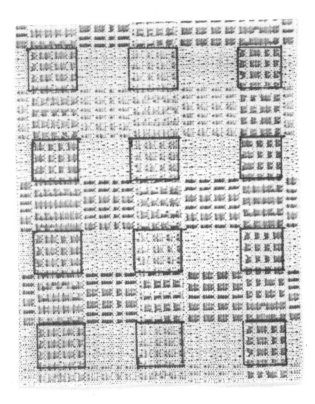

Figure 21.   A Bunting.
A. Envision a quilt-stitching scheme based on the plaid, so that all you will have to do is sew over certain of the plaid's lines. Leave unquilted the area within 1 inch of the outside edges.

safety pins as you come to them. *Don't try to sew over safety pins.* Proceed carefully and stop periodically to place a hand above and a hand below the quilt to smooth out wrinkles along the quilting line. Begin and end every line of quilt stitching by taking three to five stitches in place. Remember to leave the outside inch on every side unquilted.

Lay the quilted square on the floor. Fold the two unsewn edges toward the center as shown in Figure 21B. Pin the left edge of the *closed* zipper between the two layers of flannel on the unsewn edge of the quilt to the left of the zipper. While the zipper is still closed, pin the zipper's right half between the layers of flannel on the unsewn edge of the quilt to the zipper's right. Then open the zipper and, using a zipper foot, a stitch length of 12 (2.5 for metric machines), and a still slightly loosened presser-foot pressure setting, sew the zipper halves in place. Topstitch around the rest of the perimeter of the quilt, ⅛ inch from the edge, with a regular presser foot but the same stitch length and presser-foot pressure settings.

That's it. Use the warm and gentle cycles to wash this quilt; dry it alternately on permanent press and fluff settings. Do not line-dry or press this or any other quilt.

Figure 21 continued

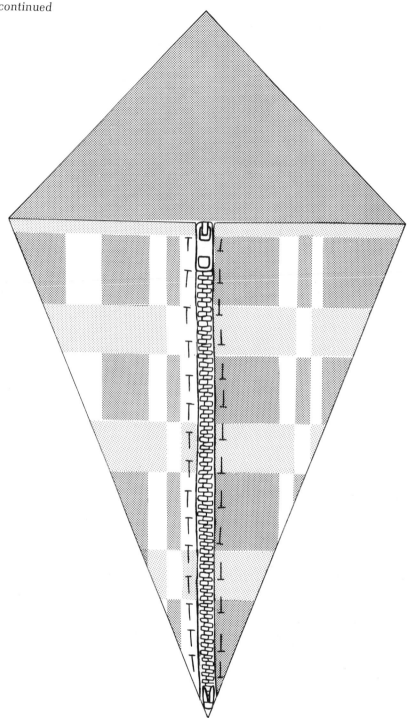

B. To pin the zipper in place, fold the quilt like a bunting and lay each edge of the *closed* **zipper between the two layers of flannel along an unsewn edge of the quilt.**

Border-Print Bedspread (QQQ)

Border-print fabric lends symmetry to this ruffled bedspread and matching pillow sham(s). Directions for four bed sizes are given. To make this design, you will need:

- border-print fabric at least 42 inches wide (if the bed is higher than 20¾ inches above the floor, the fabric must be wider): 14½ yards for full, 13⅛ yards for twin, 15⅛ yards for extra-long full, or 13¾ yards for extra-long twin
- 4-ounce *bonded* polyester batting: 5⅛ square yards for full; 2⅞ for twin; 4½ for extra-long full; or 3¼ for extra-long twin
- thick cording: 5⅞ yards for full, 5½ yards for twin, 6⅛ yards for extra-long full, or 5¾ yards for extra-long twin
- one flat twin sheet (for all sizes)
- a sewing machine with a size 9 or 11 (European size 65 or 75) needle, a quilting guide (a 6-inch quilting guide if the border of the print is not contained within a panel), a zipper foot, and a quilting foot
- a Bishop hem guide (Dritz® Ezy-Hem® Guide)
- an ironing board and an iron
- a yardstick
- a washable ink marker
- common pins
- 50 or so large (1½-inch) safety pins (reusable)
- fabric shears
- a seam ripper

Remove one hem from the sheet. Prewash and dry the fabric and the sheet by machine.

Consult Figure 22A and select the appropriate scheme for cutting the fabric (see also fabric requirements and "Quilt Sizes," page 5). Begin by using the washable marker to delineate a segment—4 yards 9 inches long for full and twin sizes; 4 yards 19 inches long for extra-long full and extra-long twin. *Along the border edge* measure and mark points: 28 inches away from the segment's lower (the border) edge for full and extra-long full sizes; 20½ inches away for twin and extra-long twin. Connect these points with the measuring stick and the washable marker. Cut on the marked lines.

Fold the segment in half widthwise, press on the fold line, and cut on the crease. Place the two halves right sides together and pin along the long non-border edge. Sew a ½-inch (1.2-cm) seam, using a stitch length of 12 (2.5 for metric machines). Press the seam allowances open. This will be the quilt top. Set it aside.

From the remaining fabric, *along the border edge*, mark a length 8 yards 21 inches for full, 8 yards for twin, 9 yards for extra-long full, or 8⅜ yards for extra-long twin, to be the bed ruffles. Now measure the distance from the top of the mattress to the floor. Measure this same distance plus ¼ inch (½ inch, if the copyright information is printed conspicuously on the selvage) up from the lower (the border) edge of the segment at several intervals; mark with the washable marker. Connect the marks using the measuring stick and the marker. Cut on this line. Now cut this segment into three lengths: for full, two 113½-inch lengths and one 82-inch length; for twin, two 113½-inch lengths and one 59½-inch length; for extra-long full, two 121-inch lengths and

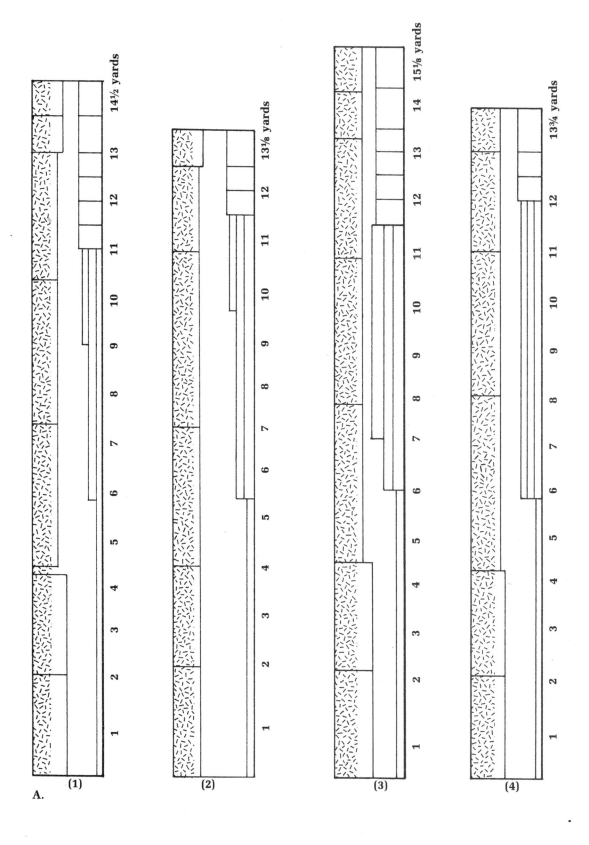

A.

(1)   14½ yards

(2)   13⅛ yards

(3)   15⅝ yards

(4)   13¾ yards

one 82-inch length; or, for extra-long twin, two 121-inch lengths and one 59½-inch length.

Mark the bed ruffles' quarter divisions by folding each of the three pieces in half widthwise with wrong sides together. With the washable marker mark the fold at the upper edge on the right side of the fabric. Unfold the fabric. Now fold each end to the center mark, wrong sides together; mark the folds, again on the upper edge on the right sides of the fabric. Make sure the marks extend at least ¾ inch (1.8 cm) inside the raw edge.

Finish the upper and the side edges of each of the three pieces by turning the edges under ¼ inch (0.6 cm) and topstitching with a stitch length of 9 (3 for metric machines) and a normal presser-foot pressure setting. On the sides but not on the upper edges, turn the edges under another ¼ inch (0.6 cm) and topstitch again. If the copyright information is printed conspicuously on the lower selvage, finish the lower edge by turning it under ¼ inch (0.6 cm) once and topstitching. Using a basting stitch of 6 (4 for metric machines), sew gathering threads ½ inch (1.2 cm) and ¾ inch (1.8 cm) from the upper edges. Do not clip the ends of the gathering threads. Set the ruffle pieces aside.

Now measure and mark fabric to cover the cording. Along the non-border selvage measure and mark with the washable marker a strip 1½ inches wide, and 5 yards 31½ inches long, for full; 5½ yards for twin; 6 yards 4½ inches for extra-long full; and 5 yards 27 inches for extra-long twin. Cut out the strip. Fold the strip in half lengthwise with wrong sides together; press in a crease. Lay the cording inside the fabric along the crease, beginning 1 inch from an end. Using a stitch-length setting of 9 (3 for metric machines) and the zipper foot, sew as close to the cording as possible. Set aside the covered cordings.

Figure 22.   Border Print Bedspread. (See opposite page.)
A. (1) Layout scheme for full-size bed (shown on 48-inch-wide material) clockwise from upper left: the two quilt top halves, each 28 inches wide and 2 yards 4½ inches long; the two side bed ruffles, each 113½ inches long and as wide as the height of the bed plus ¼ inch (½ inch if the copyright information is printed conspicuously on the border selvage); the end ruffle, which is the same width and 82 inches long; the two pillow sham fronts, each 21 × 27 inches; the two facing pieces for the sham fronts, each also 21 × 27 inches; the four sham back pieces, each 17½ × 21 inches; three lengths of 6-inch-wide pillow sham ruffle pieces; and, to cover the cording, a strip 5 yards 31½ inches long and 1½ inches wide, cut along the non-border selvage.
   (2) Layout scheme for twin (shown on 48-inch-wide fabric), clockwise from upper left: the two quilt top halves, each 20½ inches wide and 2 yards 4½ inches long; the two side bed ruffles, each 113½ inches long and as wide as the height of the bed plus ¼ inch (½ inch if the copyright information is printed conspicuously on the border selvage); the end bed ruffle, which is the same width and 59½ inches long; the pillow sham front, which is 21 × 27 inches; the facing piece for the sham front, also 21 × 27 inches; the two sham back pieces, each 17½ × 21-inches; the 6-inch-wide sham ruffle; and, to cover the cording, a strip 5½ yards long and 1½ inches wide, cut along the non-border selvage.
   (3) Layout scheme for extra-long full (shown on 48-inch-wide material), clockwise from upper left: the two quilt top halves, each 28 inches wide and 2 yards 9½ inches long; the two side bed ruffles, each 121 inches long and as wide as the height of the bed plus ¼ inch (½ inch if the copyright information is printed conspicuously on the border selvage); the end bed ruffle, which is the same width and 82 inches long; the two pillow sham fronts, each 21 × 27 inches; the two facing pieces for the sham fronts, each also 17½ × 21 inches; the four sham back pieces, each 17½ × 21 inches; three lengths of 6-inch-wide pillow sham ruffle pieces; and, to cover the cording, a strip 6 yards 4½ inches long and 1½ inches wide, cut along the non-border selvage.
   (4) Layout scheme for extra-long twin (shown on 48-inch-wide material), clockwise from upper left: the two quilt top halves, each 20½ inches wide and 2 yards 9½ inches long; the two side bed ruffles, each 121 inches long and as wide as the height of the bed plus ¼ inch (½ inch if the copyright information is printed conspicuously on the border selvage); the end bed ruffle, which is the same width and 59½ inches wide; the pillow sham front, 21 × 27 inches; the facing piece for the sham front, also 21 × 27 inches; the two sham back pieces, each 17½ × 21 inches; the 6-inch-wide sham ruffle; and, to cover the cording, a strip 5 yards 27 inches long and 1½ inches wide, cut along the non-border selvage.

Cut two (only *one* for twin sizes) 27 × 21-inch rectangle(s) along the *border edge* to serve as front pieces for the pillow shams. The border should run the length of these rectangles. Then cut the following from the remaining *non-border* portions of the fabric: four (*two* for twin sizes) sham ruffles, each 6 inches wide and 6 yards long. Use the sham front pieces as patterns for cutting two (one for twin sizes) sham front facing piece(s), each 21 × 27 inches. Finally cut four (*two* for twin) sham backs, each 17½ × 21 inches.

Mark the quarter divisions along the sides and foot of the quilt top. First fold the quilt in half widthwise with wrong sides together; pin and press in a crease. Then fold the upper and lower edges to the crease, wrong sides together, and mark the fold lines with the washable marker. On the lower edge of the quilt top, fold the left and right edges to the seam, wrong sides together; mark the folds. Be sure that all of these markings extend ¾ inch inside the raw edges.

Now use the washable marker to delineate the quilt-stitching lines shown in Figure 22B. These will serve as guides for subsequent, parallel rows of quilt stitching. *If the border is contained within a panel,* begin by marking points along the upper edge of the panel, 3 inches to the left and the right of the quilt top's center crease. At each point, construct a 3-inch line perpendicular to the panel. Use the measuring stick and the marker to connect the ends of these lines, forming an "X" from one edge to the other across the quilt.

If the fabric's border is not contained within a panel, mark points 4 inches to the left and the right of the center crease along the outside edges. At each point, construct a 6-inch-long line perpendicular to the edge. Use the measuring stick and the marker to connect the ends of these lines, forming an "X" across the quilt.

Use the Bishop hem guide to press under ½ inch along the upper edge of the quilt top.

Lay the quilt top on the floor and cut and piece the batting to conform to its dimensions. Set the quilt top and the batting aside and lay the sheet wrong side up on the floor. Smooth out any wrinkles. Center the batting over the sheet so that there are at least 2 inches of sheet showing on every side. Lay the quilt top, right side up, over the batting. *Without lifting the quilt,* secure all three layers together with well-spaced safety pins.

Quilt, beginning at the center seam and working to the outside edges. Loosen the presser-foot pressure slightly; use a quilting foot and a stitch length of 9 (3 for metric machines). Lower the needle into the intersection of the center seam and the crease. With the stitch length temporarily set on zero, take three to five stitches in place. Then simply sew over one of the marked quilting lines. Remove safety pins as you come to them; *don't try to sew over safety pins.* Stop ⅛ inch (0.3 cm) short of the edge of the panel, if there is a panel (if there is no panel, quilt to the edges of the fabric). Set the stitch length at zero and take another three to five stitches in place. Beginning at the center, sew over each of the other three marked quilting lines, stitching in place at the start and the end of every line.

Use the quilting guide at a 3-inch setting if the border is contained within a panel (at a 4-inch setting if there is no panel) for the remaining rows of quilt stitching. Simply begin each new row at the center seam and quilt parallel to, and 3 inches (4 inches if there's no panel) distant from, the preceding row of quilt stitching. Quilt to the outside edges of the quilt, leaving unquilted the last ½ inch (1.2 cm) of the upper (the pressed) edge. Then, if there is a panel, quilt-stitch along the panel's *outside* edge, ⅛ inch (0.3 cm) away.

Now trim the edges of the sheet even with the edges of the quilt top. Along the upper (the pressed) edge, trim the sheet ½ inch (1.2 cm) beyond the crease, even with the raw edge of the quilt top.

Lay the fabric-covered cording along the quilt top's side and lower edges, with right sides together. Beginning at the upper edge, pin the non-selvage seam allowance of the cording to the raw edges of the quilt top, leaving at least ½ inch (1.2 cm) of empty casing extending beyond the upper edge (the fold). With the presser-foot pressure still slightly loosened, use a stitch length of 9 (3 for metric machines) and a zipper foot to sew as close to the cording as possible. You should

Figure 22 continued

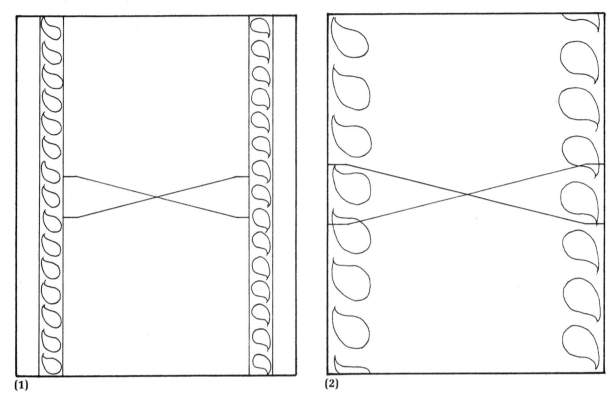

(1)   **(2)**

B. (1) Mark these quilt-stitching lines if the border is contained inside a panel. Then quilt in rows 3 inches distant from and parallel to the marked lines, beginning in the center of the quilt, and working to the outside. Then quilt-stitch a line parallel to and ⅛ inch (0.3 cm) from the outside edge of each border.

(2) Mark these quilt-stitching lines if the border is *not* contained within a panel. Then quilt in rows 4 inches distant from and parallel to the marked lines, beginning in the center of the quilt and working to the outside.

be able to sew along the seam in the fabric covering the cord. Begin ½ inch (1.2 cm) from the upper (the pressed) edge of the quilt top; sew around that side, the lower edge, and the other side, stopping ½ inch (1.2 cm) from the upper edge.

Tuck the ends of the cording's casing between the top and bottom layers of the quilt top. Finger-press the sheet's upper edge to the inside; pin. Topstitch over the upper edge of the quilt top, using the quilting foot and a stitch length of 12 (2.5 for metric machines), with the presser-foot pressure still slightly loosened.

Pin the ruffles, right sides up, over the right side of the cording's selvage seam allowance, matching quarter divisions. Gather and pin. Use a normal presser-foot pressure setting, a zipper foot, and a stitch length of 12 (2.5 for metric machines) to topstitch the upper edges of the ruffles to the seam allowance—as close to the cording as possible.

Remove the gathering threads. To remove the washable ink lines, launder the quilted bedspread on a warm and gentle washing machine cycle (or according to the manufacturer's instructions), dry it alternately on warm and fluff settings. Press the ruffles if necessary, but *do not iron* the quilted portion of this or any other quilt.

Pillow Shams for the Border-Print Bedspread (QQQ)

To mark the quilt-stitching lines on the border-print pillow-sham fronts (one front only for twin), first fold the sham front pieces in half widthwise and press in a crease. If the border is contained inside a panel, use the washable ink marker to mark points 3 inches to each side of the crease, along the upper edge of the panel. Using the Bishop hem guide, construct straight lines at these points, 3 inches long and perpendicular to the edge of the panel. Connect the ends of these lines with the center crease at the upper edge of the fabric. See Figure 23A, layout (1).

Layout (2) of Figure 23A shows the marked quilting lines for pillow shams made of border-print fabric on which the border is *not* contained within a panel. At the lower edge of the sham, measure and mark points 4 inches to either side of the center crease. Then, using the Bishop hem guide, construct straight lines at these points, 6 inches long and perpendicular to the edge of the sham. Connect the ends of these two lines with the center crease at the upper edge of the fabric.

Use a sham front piece as a pattern to cut two pieces (one piece only for twin) of batting. Then lay each sham front facing wrong side up on a flat surface; smooth out any wrinkles. Over it lay a rectangle of batting. Lay a border-print sham-front rectangle over the batting. *Without lifting the fabrics*, secure all three layers together with a few well-spaced large safety pins.

To do the quilt stitching, loosen the presser-foot pressure slightly and set the stitch-length adjustment for 9 (3 for metric machines). Use the quilting foot. Lower the needle into the center crease along the upper edge, and, with the stitch-length regulator temporarily set on zero, take three to five stitches in place. Quilt over a marked quilting line to ⅛ inch short of the upper edge of the panel (or to the lower edge of the fabric if there is no panel); remove any safety pins in your path. *Don't try to sew over safety pins*. Take another three to five stitches in place to finish the row. Beginning at the upper edge again, quilt-stitch over the other marked quilting line, stitching in place at the beginning and end.

Use the quilting guide at the 3-inch setting (at a 4-inch setting if there is no panel) for the remaining rows of quilt stitching. Simply begin each row at the upper edge of the sham and quilt parallel to and 3 inches (4 inches is there's no panel) distant from the preceding row of quilt stitching. Quilt to ⅛ inch (0.3 cm) above the top of the panel (to the edge of the fabric if there is no panel), remembering to *remove safety pins* as you come to them. Stitch in place to begin and end every row of quilt stitching. Then, if there is a panel, quilt-stitch along the panel's upper and lower edges, ⅛ inch outside its edges.

To form the ruffles, pin the two ends of each 6-inch-wide strip together, right sides facing, to form a loop. With the presser-foot pressure on a normal setting, sew, using a ¼-inch (0.6-cm) seam and a stitch-length setting of 12 (2.5 for metric machines). Press the seam allowances open. Then fold each ruffle in half lengthwise, wrong sides together, and press. To mark the quarter divisions, fold the ruffle on the seam; use the washable marker to mark the fold at the opposite end. Now align the seam and the mark with each other, and mark the folds at both sides. With the stitch-length regulator set at 6 (4 for metric machines), sew two rows of gathering stitches ¼ inch (0.6 cm) and ⅜ inch (0.9 cm) away from the raw edges of the ruffles, through both layers. *Don't clip the ends of the gathering threads.*

Fold each sham front in half lengthwise with wrong sides together; use a washable marker to mark the folds on the left and right sides. Pin the ruffles to the right sides of the sham fronts, matching the quarter divisions of the ruffles to the washable marks on the sides and to the creases on the upper and the lower edges. The folded edges of the ruffles should face inward (Figure 23B). Gather the ruffles by pulling the gathering threads gently; pin. Using a stitch length of 6 (4

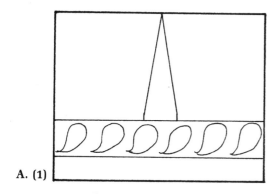

A. (1)

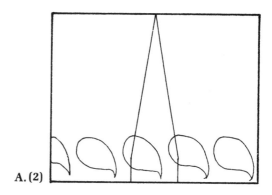

A. (2)

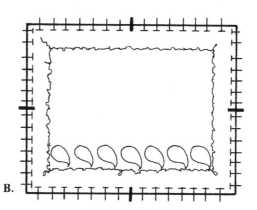

B.

Figure 23.   Pillow Shams for the Border-Print Bedspread.
A. (1) **Marked quilt-stitching lines on a border-print sham with a panel.**
   (2) **Marked quilt-stitching lines on a border-print sham with the border not contained within a panel.**
B. **Pin the ruffle to the right side of the sham front, matching the quarter divisions. The folded edge of the ruffle should face inward.**

for metric machines) and a slightly loosened presser-foot pressure, baste the ruffles to the fronts with a ½-inch (1.2-cm) seam.

Finish one 21-inch edge of each sham back piece by turning the raw edge under ¼ inch (0.6 cm) and topstitching over it, then turning the edge under another ¼ inch (0.6 cm) and topstitching again. Use a normal presser-foot pressure setting and a stitch length of 9 (3 for metric machines).

Lay the pillow sham backs over the fronts, right sides together. The finished edges of the two back pieces will overlap each other by about 4 inches. Pin. Sew permanently around the entire perimeter with a stitch length of 12 (2.5 for metric machines) and a ½-inch (1.2-cm) seam.

Follow the manufacturer's instructions for washing, or launder on warm and gentle cycles to remove the washable ink lines.

Prequilted Bedspread (QQQQ)

This is an even simpler version of the design used in Border-Print Bedspread. It is easily adaptable to beds—twin or extra-long twin—that are unusually high or low. Directions for making pillow shams are included.

Fabric amounts do *not* include allowances for preshrinking. You will need:

- 2¾ (2⅞ for extra-long twin) yards of double-faced, prequilted fabric at least 40 inches wide, for the quilt and the pillow sham front
- 8 (8⅜ for extra-long twin) yards of unquilted fabric at least as wide as the height of the bed plus 1 inch, for the bed ruffles
- ⅝ yard of fabric 36 inches wide, or ½ yard of fabric 42 inches wide (or wider), of unquilted fabric for the pillow sham backs
- 2 yards 24½ inches of ruffle for the pillow sham
- 5⅜ yards of large piping
- 1⅛ yards of double-fold bias tape
- thread
- a sewing machine with a size 9 or 11 (European size 65 or 75) needle and a zipper foot
- a Bishop hem guide (Dritz® Ezy-Hem® Guide)
- an ironing board and an iron
- a yardstick
- a washable marker
- common pins
- fabric shears

Prewash and dry fabrics by machine.

Cut a 40 × 76-inch (40 × 81-inch for extra-long twin) rectangle from the double-faced, prequilted fabric. With the washable ink marker, delineate quarter divisions along the rectangle's side edges and lower edge. These marks will facilitate ruffle placement. First fold the rectangle in half with wrong sides together; mark the fold at least ¾ inch inside the raw edge of the fabric. Then fold left and right edges to the center mark, wrong sides together, and mark the folds at least ¾ inch inside the raw edges of the fabric.

Measure the distance from the top of the mattress to the floor. Measure this same distance plus ¾ inch (1 inch if the copyright information is printed conspicuously on the selvage) up from the lower edge of the bed-ruffle fabric at several intervals; mark with the washable marker. Connect the marks, using the yardstick and the marker. Cut on this line. Then cut two segments of this bed-ruffle fabric, each 113½ inches long (121 inches for extra-long twin), and one ruffle segment 59½ inches long.

Mark the ruffles' quarter divisions by folding each of the three pieces in half lengthwise with wrong sides together. Use the washable marker to mark the fold at the upper edge, on the right side of the fabric. Unfold the fabric. Now fold each end to the center mark, wrong sides together, and mark the folds on the upper edge, on the right side of the fabric. These marks should extend at least ¾ inch inside the raw edge of the fabric.

Slide the fabric back along one end of the piping, exposing the cording; cut off ½ inch of the

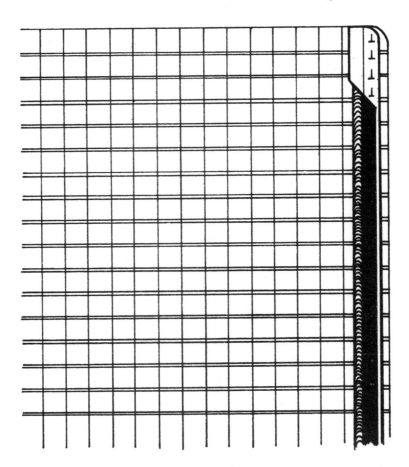

Figure 24.   Prequilted Bedspread.
A. Pin one of the seam allowances of the piping to the side and the lower edge of the prequilted fabric, right sides together.

cording and pull the fabric back to its original position. Beginning with the cordless half-inch, pin one of the piping's seam allowances to the side and the lower edges of the prequilted rectangle, right sides together (Figure 24A). At the other end, push back the fabric of the piping and cut the cording ½ inch short of the end of the quilt.

Sew the piping to the prequilted rectangle, using a zipper foot and a stitch length of 9 (3 for metric machines). Leave the presser-foot pressure slightly loosened. Sew as close to the cording as possible; you should be able to sew along the seam of the piping.

Encase the upper edge of the quilt and the ends of the piping's casing in double-fold bias tape. Topstitch with the presser-foot pressure still slightly loosened and with the stitch-length regulator set at 9 (3 for metric machines). Then use the Bishop hem guide to press under the edge ½ inch (1.2 cm). Pin and topstitch again ⅜ inch (0.9 cm) from the edge.

Finish the upper and side edges of the side pieces and the end piece by turning the edges under ¼ inch (0.6 cm); topstitch with a stitch length of 9 (3 for metric machines) and a normal presser-foot pressure setting. If the copyright information is printed conspicuously on the lower selvage, finish the lower edge by turning it under ¼ inch (0.6 cm) *once* and topstitching. On the *sides*, but *not on the upper edges*, turn the edges under another ¼ inch (0.6 cm) and topstitch again.

Figure 24 continued

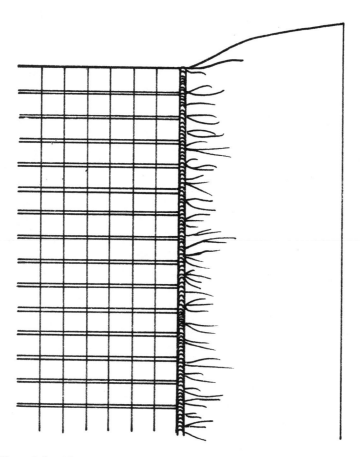

B. Pin the ruffles, right sides up, to the right side of the piping's remaining seam allowance.

Using a basting stitch of 6 (4 for metric machines), sew gathering threads ½ inch (1.2 cm) and ¾ inch (1.8 cm) from the upper edges. *Do not clip the ends of the gathering threads.*

Pin the ruffles, right sides up, to the right side of the remaining seam allowance of the piping, matching the quarter divisions (Figure 24B). Gather and pin. Use a normal presser-foot pressure setting, a zipper foot, and a stitch length of 12 (2.5 for metric machines) to topstitch the upper edges of the ruffles to the seam allowance of the piping—as close to the cording as possible.

Remove the gathering threads. To remove the washable ink lines, follow the manufacturer's instructions, or launder the quilted bedspread on a warm and gentle washing cycle and dry it alternately on warm and fluff settings. Press the bed ruffles, if necessary, but *do not iron* the quilted portion of this or any other quilt.

Prequilted Shams (QQQQ)

From the double-faced, prequilted remnant, cut a rectangular sham front piece 21 × 27 inches. Cut two rectangles, each 17 × 21 inches, from the unquilted material to serve as sham back pieces.

Pin the ends of the ruffle together, right sides together, forming a loop. Sew, using a ¼-inch (0.6 cm) seam and a stitch-length setting of 12 (2.5 for metric machines). Press the seam allowances open. Pin the ruffle to the prequilted sham front, right sides together, with the ruffle facing the center of the rectangle. See Figure 25. Loosen the presser-foot pressure slightly, set the stitch-length regulator for 6 (4 for metric machines), and baste the ruffle to the sham front with a ½-inch (1.2-cm) seam.

Finish one edge of each of the two sham back pieces by turning the raw edge under ¼ inch (0.6 cm), topstitching over it, turning the raw edge under another ¼ inch (0.6 cm), and topstitching again.

Lay the pillow sham backs over the fronts, right sides together. The backs will overlap each other by about 4 inches in the center. Pin. Permanently sew the backs, the fronts, and the ruffles together with a stitch length of 12 (2.5 for metric machines) and a ½-inch (1.2-cm) seam.

Clip the seam and trim the corners. Turn the pillow sham right side out. Launder on warm and gentle settings.

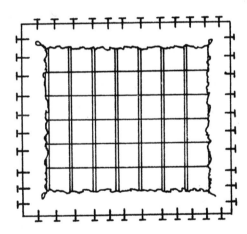

Figure 25. Pin the ruffle to the right side of the sham front, with the ruffle facing inward.

Granddaughter's Flower Garden (QQ)

Grandmother's Flower Garden was never like this. This coverlet, instead of using hundreds of tiny hexagons, uses a few large, prestuffed ones. Because each hexagon is quilted (by machine, of course) before being connected to the others, and because the hexagons are added one at a time around a central hexagon, a coverlet this size is easily manageable by machine. Possibly the best news of all is that there is only one pattern piece.

You will need:

- cotton fabric with a smooth, tight weave for top and bottom hexagon pieces (this quilt provides an ideal opportunity to use the pretty scraps you've saved—but use *only* unworn fabric. You may want to arrange the hexagons in concentric rings of the same color, or use a random color scheme; both are traditional.)
- 5½ square yards of 5-ounce *bonded* polyester batting
- 4 yards of quilt binding
- thread (four large spools for the quilt stitching and the satin stitching, plus thread to match the quilt binding)
- a sewing machine with a size 9 or 11 (European size 65 or 75) needle, a zigzag attachment, and a quilting foot
- an ironing board and an iron
- a yardstick
- a pencil
- paper
- pattern weights
- a large compass, or a pencil on a string
- a washable marker
- common pins
- at least 24 large (1½-inch) safety pins (reusable)
- paper-cutting scissors
- fabric shears

Prewash and dry the fabrics by machine.

Make the pattern piece: construct a circle with a radius of 9¾ inches. Using the same compass setting, place the pivot leg of the compass on any point on the edge of the circle and draw an arc through the circle's circumference. Now place the pivot leg of the compass on the point at which the arc intersects the circumference; make a second arc. Continue making arcs around the circle until you return to the starting point. Connect the intersection points to form a hexagon (see Figure 26A).

Use the paper pattern to cut 23 hexagons for the quilt top. Hold the pattern in place with pattern weights. If you are using striped fabric for one of the rings of hexagons, match the stripes by cutting out the first striped hexagon and then using it as a pattern for the remaining ones (Figure 26B); lay it right side up over the fabric and align its stripes with those of the fabric. (Figure 26F shows one arrangement for striped hexagons.)

Use the yardstick and the pencil to bisect the pattern. Draw a line ¼ inch away from and parallel to this bisecting line. *Do not cut on this line;* fold the smaller "half" of the pattern under

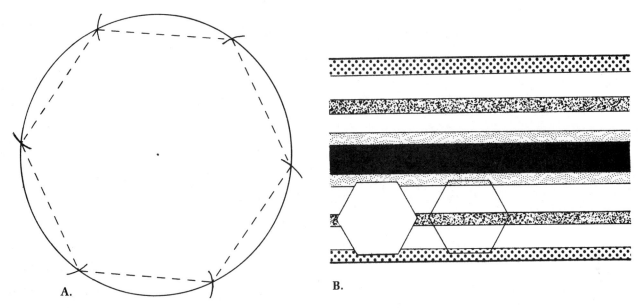

Figure 26.   Granddaughter's Flower Garden.
A. Make the hexagon pattern by constructing a circle 9¾ inches in radius; use the same compass setting to intersect the circle's circumference six times. Connect the intersection points with a straightedge.
B. To match the stripes in a ring of striped hexagons, use the paper pattern to cut the first striped piece, and then use that piece as a pattern for the remaining pieces. Simply lay the fabric "pattern" right side up over the fabric so that its stripes align with those of the fabric.

on this line, and use the larger "half" as a pattern for the four half-hexagons of the quilt top.

For the quilt bottom, cut 23 hexagons and 4 half-hexagons. Cut 23 hexagons and 4 half-hexagons from the batting.

Make each prestuffed unit by pinning a quilt-top piece to its counterpart on the quilt bottom, right sides together. Lay both pieces over a batting piece. Remove the pins one at a time and replace them through all three layers. Release the pressure on the presser-foot slightly. With the batting facing downward, sew a ¼-inch (0.6-cm) seam around five sides and the first inch and last inch of the sixth side; use a stitch length of 9 (3 for metric machines). Turn each hexagon right side out through the opening in the sixth side.

NOTE: Before you sew, consult Figure 26C. Leave the outside edges of the half-hexagons and pieces 7 and 8 completely unsewn. The open edge of a 4 or a 5 piece should *not* be an outside edge.

Press each prestuffed piece flat, with the seams exactly at the edges. Press the raw edges (except on the half-hexagons and pieces 7 and 8) under ¼ inch; pin and topstitch very near the edge.

Mark the quilt-stitching lines with the washable ink marker (Figure 26D). Lay the yardstick across each hexagon, from each corner to the directly opposite corner; mark. Mark the two quilt-stitching lines on the half-hexagons (Figure 26E); they run from the inside corners to the midway point on the outside edge.

For the quilt stitching leave the stitch-length adjustment at 9 (3 for metric machines) and the presser-foot pressure slightly loosened. Lower the needle into a marked quilting line at a corner. Temporarily set the stitch-length adjustment at zero and take three to five stitches in place.

Figure 26 continued

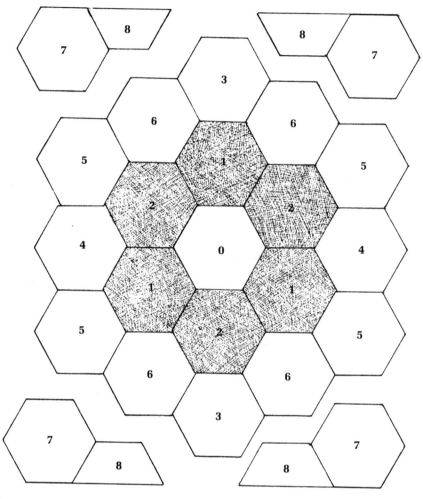

C. The numbers indicate the sequence in which the prestuffed units are sewn together around the central hexagon (0).

To connect the prestuffed and prequilted units, start with the central hexagon. Lay a 1 hexagon against the central hexagon without overlapping the two. With large safety pins "baste" them together (see Figure 26D). Then satin-stitch them by following the satin-stitching instructions in the owner's manual of your sewing machine; or use the zigzag presser foot, a stitch length of 20 (0.5 for metric machines), and your widest zigzag stitch. Remove the safety pins as you come to them. *Don't try to sew over safety pins.* To prevent the sewing machine from jamming, hold the excess top threads in your hand and pull them taut toward the back of the sewing machine as you take three to five stitches in place (with the stitch-length setting temporarily on zero) and then a few stitches forward. Safety-pin-baste the other two 1 hexagons to the central hexagon and satin-stitch them. Then safety-pin-baste and satin-stitch the 2 hexagons to the 0 and the 1's. Add the remaining pieces in the order indicated by the numbering scheme in the illustration. The satin stitching should hide the topstitching on the sixth side of each hexagon.

Figure 26 continued

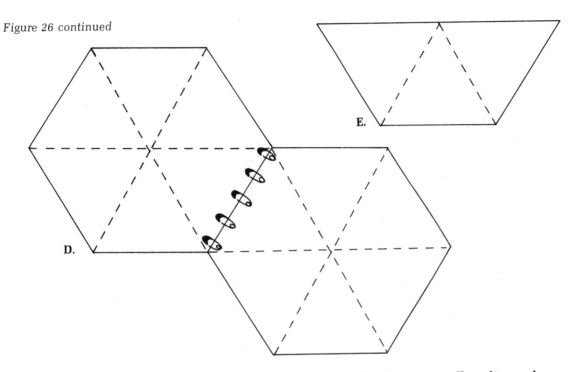

D. One prestuffed hexagon is basted to another with safety pins; the edges are not allowed to overlap. The broken lines indicate quilt-stitching lines.
E. Quilt-stitching lines on a half-hexagon unit.

When all the prestuffed units are connected, topstitch over the side ("scalloped") edges of the quilt. Use a straight stitch and a stitch length of 12 (2.5 for metric machines). Leave the presser-foot pressure in a slightly relaxed position.

Then apply quilt binding to the head and the foot (the straight) edges only. Begin by cutting the end of the quilt binding at a 60-degree angle (the angle of the corner of the quilt). Press the end of the binding under ¼ inch. Encase the upper edge of the quilt inside the quilt binding and pin it in place. Cut the quilt binding at least ¼ inch longer than the edge of the quilt—at a 60-degree angle. Finger-press the end under ¼ inch. Finish pinning the quilt binding to the quilt's upper edge. With the presser-foot pressure still slightly loosened and the stitch-length adjustment still set for 12 (2.5 for metric machines), straight-stitch two rows, ⅛ and ¼ inch from the inside edge of the binding. Apply binding to the quilt's lower edge in the same way.

That's it. A trip through the washing machine (on the warm and gentle cycle, or as recommended by the manufacturer) will remove the washable ink markings. Machine-dry the quilt alternately on warm and fluff settings.

Variation of Granddaughter's Flower Garden (QQQ)

Mark the quilt-stitching lines in a Star of David configuration, as shown in Figure 27. For the half-hexagons, draw lines connecting the inside corner with the opposite, outside corners. Then connect the inside corners to points on the outside edge, $4^9/_{10}$ inches from the corners.

Figure 26 continued

F. Granddaughter's Flower Garden with a ring of striped hexagons.

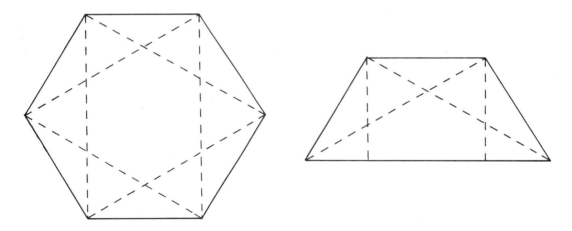

Figure 27.   Quilt-stitching lines for the Star of David variation.

Woven Coverlet (Q)

The texture of this reversible 85 × 63-inch coverlet is so intriguing that you may want to redecorate the bedroom around the quilt. Machine quilting in X's leaves the edges of the woven strands unfettered, showing off the many layers that allow the coverlet to trap air for warmth without weight. If you don't want to redecorate, the quilt can easily coordinate with your existing color scheme; it's made from bed sheets.

To make this coverlet you will need:

- four new flat twin sheets NOTE: the sheets must be at least 66 inches wide *after* preshrinking
- 8¾ square yards of 3.3-ounce *bonded* polyester batting
- 8½ yards of blanket binding
- thread
- a sewing machine with a size 9 or 11 (European size 65 or 75) needle, a quilting foot, and a quilting guide (optional)
- an ironing board and an iron
- a yardstick or measuring tape
- masking tape
- a washable marker
- common pins
- about 170 large (1½-inch) safety pins (reusable)
- fabric shears
- a seam ripper

Remove the hem from one end of each sheet. Wash and dry the sheets by machine.

Decide which sheets will be the "woof" (the short strands) and which the "warp" (the long strands) on both top and bottom. On the wrong side of each warp sheet draw an arrow parallel to each selvage edge with a washable marker. On the wrong side of each woof sheet draw arrows parallel to the sheet's hemmed (or once-hemmed) ends. Measure and trim the warp sheets to 85 inches in length. Measure and trim the woof sheets to a width of 66 inches.

Lay a woof sheet right side up on the floor. Lay the other woof sheet over it, wrong side up, and pin the two together, placing common pins along both long sides and one end. Smooth out any wrinkles.

Cut a piece of batting to 85 × 66 inches. If two or more sections of batting must be pieced together, be sure that the seams of the batting run in the same direction as the arrows. Lay the batting over the sheets. Remove the pins one at a time and replace them through all three layers *without lifting the sheets or the batting*. Secure the remaining end with about five safety pins.

Use masking tape to delinate 5¾- and 6¼-inch seam-guide lines on the sewing machine (Figure 28A). Loosen the pressure on the presser foot very slightly. Set the stitch-length adjustment for 9 (3 for metric machines).

Fold the safety-pinned end of the sheets and the batting 8 inches over the rest. Roll the fabrics to within a foot of the opposite end.

With the batting facing downward, stitch a seam ¼ inch (0.6 cm) from the end pinned with common pins (*all seams are in the direction of the arrows*). Make the second and third seams 5¾ and 6¼ inches, respectively, from the edge. After the third seam has been sewn, write 1 with a

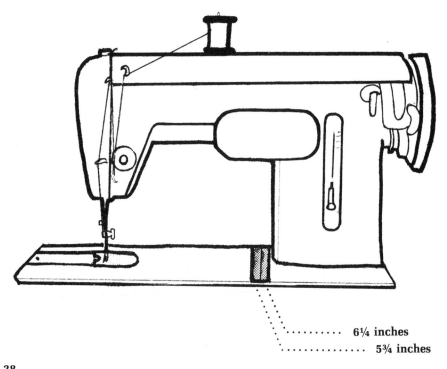

6¼ inches

5¾ inches

Figure 28.
A. Use masking tape to make seam-guide lines on the sewing machine, 5¾ and 6¼ inches away from the needle.

washable marker on the top sheet's right side at the beginning of the seam. If neither the top nor the bottom fabric is a large print, ignore instructions to number the strands. Cut *midway* between the second and the third seams to leave ¼-inch (0.6-cm) seam allowances.

Subsequent seams alternate between 5¾ inches and 6¼ inches. After sewing two more seams, number the sewn strand and cut it off. Unroll the bundle as you work. Make fifteen "woof" strands.

Turn each strand right side out by placing a hand inside it, gathering it onto your arm, taking hold of the far end of the strand, and pulling your hand back through the tube. Press each strip flat, with the seams exactly at the sides.

Pin the ends and one selvage edge of the warp sheets right sides together on the floor. Lay an 85 × 66-inch piece of batting over them (remember that batting seams must run parallel to the arrows), remove the pins one at a time, and replace the pins through all three layers. Use safety pins on the remaining selvage edge. Fold the safety-pinned edge back 8 inches over the rest of the fabric. Roll the fabric to within 1 foot of the opposite selvage edge.

With the batting facing downward, stitch the first seam ¼ inch (0.6 cm) from the selvage edge. You could stitch the second seam 5¾ inches, and the third seam 6¼ inches, from the edge, but if either of the warp sheets is no wider than 66 inches, that would allow you no margin for error regarding seam widths. Instead, sew the second seam on the 5¾-inch seam guide line, and use a quilting guide to sew the third seam ⅜ inch (0.9 cm) from the second seam. The strands will be virtually identical width regardless of the method used.

Then number the sewn strand on the right side of the top fabric, and cut *midway* between the second and third seams. Sew subsequent seams alternately on the 5¾-inch line, and ⅜ inch (0.9 cm) from the last seam; number the strands and cut them off. Make eleven warp strands, turn them right side out, and press them.

Figure 28 continued

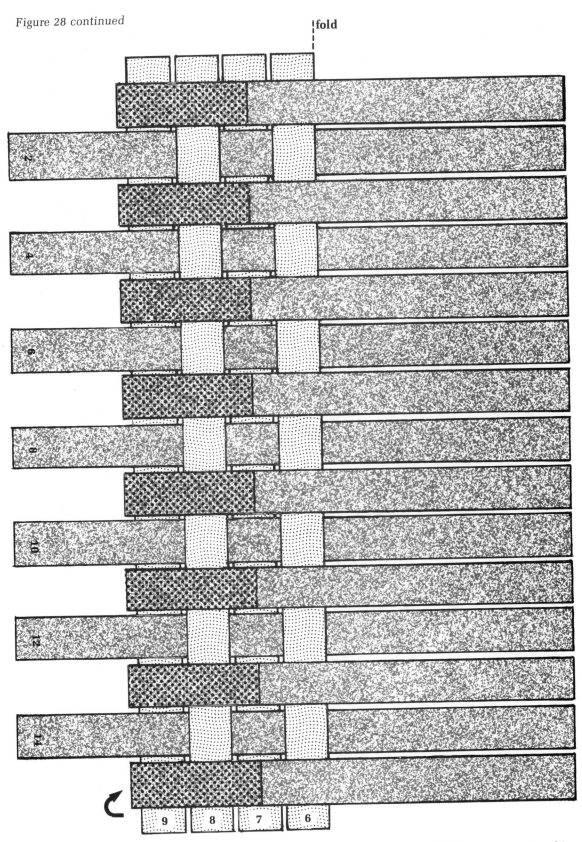

B. **Weave a checkerboard pattern by folding back every other woof strand, laying a warp strand in place, and returning the folded woof strands to the floor.**

Figure 28 continued

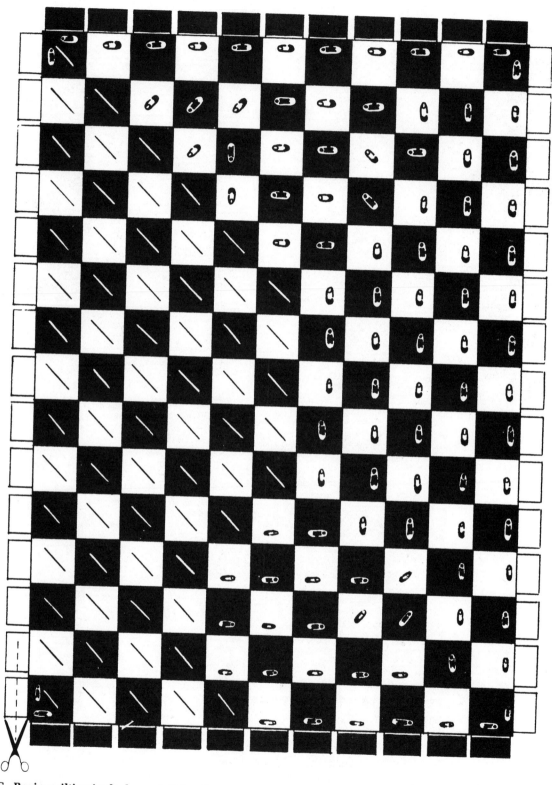

C. Begin quilting in the lower-left-hand corner, removing safety pins in your path. Quilt the diagonal lines shown; then, beginning from the lower-right-hand corner, finish the first diagonal quilting. Work from the remaining two corners to quilt the cross-diagonal lines.

Figure 28 continued

(1)

(2)

(3)

D. Three alternatives to checkerboard: Weave (1) is used with the sailboat print in Figure 29A (see page 120) and B (see page 121) (the reverse side, made with an identical sailboat print sheet). A solid-color woof and a geometric print warp are shown in Weave (2) in illustration 2. The quilt in Illustration 1 uses Weave (3).

Illustration 1

Illustration 2

If either side of the warp strands is a large print, lay the warp strands in order side by side on the floor. Determine whether the numbers should read from left to right or from right to left when the quilt top is facing upward, and make a note to that effect. Set aside the warp strands.

If either of the woof strands is a large print, determine whether the numbers should read from left to right or from right to left. Lay the woof strands on the floor in sequence, with the quilt-top fabric facing upward.

For a checkerboard weave: fold every other woof strand in "half" (actually, 3 inches beyond the halfway point) widthwise. Lay Number 6 warp strand, with the quilt-top fabric facing upward, perpendicular to the woof strands, against the folds (see Figure 28B). Return the folded woof strands to the floor over Number 6 warp strand. Fold the *other* woof strands back at the lower edge of Number 6 warp strand. Lay the next warp strand (Number 7 or Number 5, depending on whether the numbers on the warp strands read from left to right or from right to left) in place along the folds. Continue folding back woof strands and weaving in warp strands until six warp strands are woven. Then begin in the middle again and, working in the opposite direction, weave in the remaining five warp strands.

More interesting weaves are possible (see Figure 28D).

With the help of a friend or friends, straighten the weave by pulling opposite ends of the strands until they are taut and at right angles to the perpendicular strands. The sides of each strand should just touch its neighbors; there should not be overlapping of strands or gaps between them. The ends of the woof and the warp strands will extend beyond the outside of the last perpendicular strands. When you're satisfied with the tightness of the weave, pin safety pins around the quilt's edges—one on each perimeter square and two on each corner square. *Without lifting the quilt*, place a safety pin in the center of every 5½-inch square. Trim the strand end extending beyond the outside perpendicular strands to 1½ inches.

The machine quilt stitching is done in diagonal lines across each square, with no quilting on the beginning inch or the ending inch (see Figure 28C). Start on a corner square. Set the stitch-length adjustment at 9 (3 for metric machines) and loosen the presser-foot pressure slightly more. Place a hand above and a hand below the quilt to straighten both layers. Lower the needle and the presser foot. With the stitch-length adjustment temporarily on zero, take three to five stitches in place. Then sew the first diagonal, removing any safety pins in your path. *Don't try to sew over safety pins.* One inch from the lower corner, take three to five stitches in place. Quilt-stitch diagonal lines on the next four rows of squares. Then begin in the middle of the next row and stitch to the outside (see Figure 28C). Begin at the opposite corner and finish the diagonal rows. Stitch in place at the beginning and the end of every seam; stop frequently to straighten both layers with a hand above and a hand below the quilt.

Begin on a corner and quilt-stitch the "cross-diagonals" in the same manner, forming X's.

With common pins pin the blanket bonding to the strand ends that extend 1½ inches beyond the outside of the perpendicular strands. Encase the strand ends inside the binding, but leave the edges of the perpendicular strands unfettered. With a stitch-length adjustment of 10½ (2 for metric machines), topstitch on the blanket binding ¼ inch (0.6 cm) and ⅛ inch (0.3 cm) from the inside edge of the binding around the perimeter of the quilt.

Clip thread ends on both the top and the bottom. To remove markings, launder according to the manufacturer's instructions. To restore the batting's loft, dry the quilt alternately on warm and fluff settings. Do not line-dry or iron the quilted portions of this or any other quilt.

Woven Coverlet: Single-Image Variation (Q)

Many woven variations are possible. You may want to experiment with different weaves, for example. Or create a quilt with strands in three or four different fabrics per side by using solid colors or small overall prints on the woof (and/or the warp) strands and turning some of them upside down. However, don't attempt a woven quilt much larger than 85 × 63 inches, or one using batting much heavier than 3.3 ounces, because it will be unmanageable. If you elect to replace a sheet with fabric on the bolt, buy 2½ yards of fabric that is at least 66 inches wide after preshrinking.

It would be tempting to make a woven coverlet from a single-image sheet, that is, one with one big picture of, say, a sailboat or a mountain, rather than one with a repeating pattern of sailboats and mountains (see Figure 29A and 29B). Such sheets were popular about 1976—and available at designer prices.

The bad news is that single-image sheets cannot be recommended for use in quilts. Besides being expensive, they are not readily available. Moreover, they are not completely color-fast. Most sheets are roller-printed; a single-image sheet has to be screen-printed, using inks, not dyes. Some of the ink comes off every time such a sheet is laundered, causing the sheet to fade, and, more importantly, to stain everything else in the machine. Since the single-image sheet would be sewn to three other sheets, the quilt would not be machine-washable.

If, then, you are determined to incorporate a single-image sheet into a woven coverlet, proceed at your own risk. Single image sheets are expensive. They may not be available and you may have to do your own screen-printing. The quilt would not be machine-washable, and it would no longer qualify as a "quicker quilt." But it could be beautiful.

"Woven-Look" Patchwork Pillow (QQ)

You can transform a simple nine-patch design into one that mimics the texture of the woven coverlet. The difference is the quilt stitching.

Use the scraps from the sheets, two 16½-inch squares of light-colored facing fabric, two 3.3-ounce *bonded* polyester batting squares the same size, and batting remnants.

For one side of the pillow, cut five 6-inch squares from the remnant of one of the quilt top's sheets, and four 6-inch squares from the remnant of the quilt top's other sheet. Cut five 6-inch squares from one quilt-bottom sheet's remnant, and four such squares from the remnant of the other, for the pillow's reverse side. If a remnant is vertically striped, use the cutting scheme shown in Figure 30A.

Arrange the squares from the quilt-top sheets' remnants in one checkerboard pattern, the squares from the quilt-bottom sheets' remnants in another. Next, consult Figure 30B. With right sides together, pin quilt-top square 1 to quilt-top square 2, and 2 to 3; square 4 to 5, and 5 to 6; square 7 to 8, and 8 to 9. Sew, using a ¼-inch (0.6-cm) seam and a stitch length of 12 (2.5 for metric machines). Press the seam allowances open.

Then pin and sew ¼-inch (0.6-cm) seams connecting the top row to the middle row and the middle row to the bottom row. Press the seams open.

Sew the squares from the quilt bottom's remnants together in the same way.

Lay a facing square on a flat surface and smooth out any wrinkles. Lay a square of batting over it, and lay the nine-patch made from the quilt-top sheets' remnants over the batting. *Without lifting the fabric,* pin all three layers together with large safety pins.

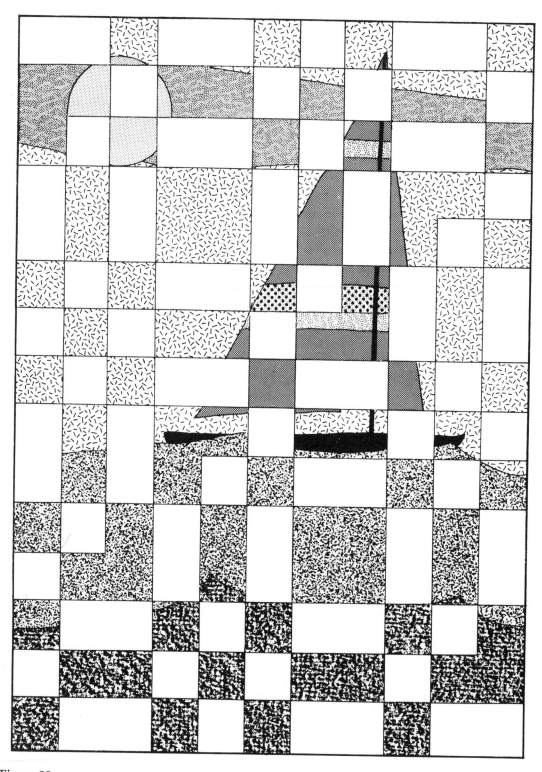

Figure 29.
A. A single-image (sailboat) sheet is incorporated into a woven coverlet, using Weave " 1 " (page 115).

Figure 29 continued

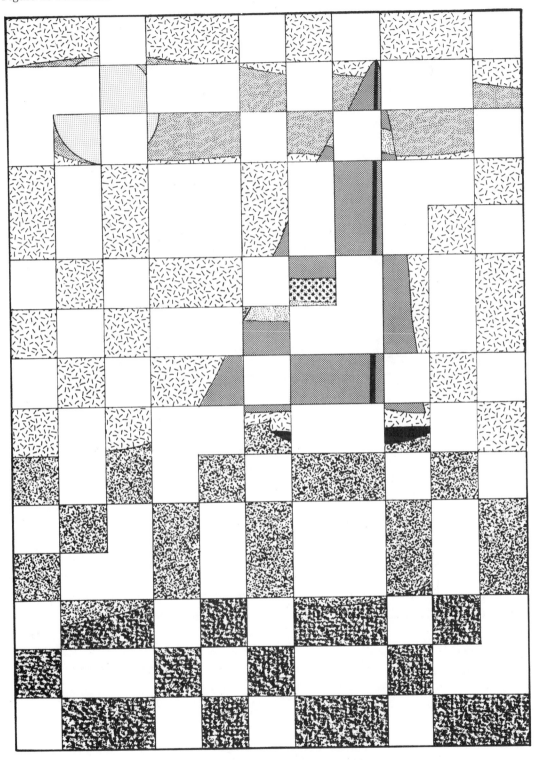

B. The reverse side of the same quilt. An identical sailboat-print sheet has been used.

The quilt stitching is done in diagonal lines across each square, with no quilting on the beginning inch or the ending inch (see Figure 30C). Set the stitch-length adjustment at 9 (3 for metric machines) and loosen the pressure on the presser foot slightly. Lower the needle and the presser foot. With the stitch-length regulator temporarily on zero, take three to five stitches in place. Then sew the first diagonal, removing any safety pins in your path. *Don't try to sew over safety pins.* One inch from the lower corner, take three to five stitches in place. Quilt-stitch diagonal lines on every square, stitching in place at the beginning and the end of every seam. Then turn the nine-patch and quilt-stitch the "cross-diagonals," forming X's.

Pin the nine-patch made from the quilt-bottom sheets' remnants to the remaining facing and batting squares; quilt-stitch the reverse side of the pillow in the same manner.

Clip thread ends.

With right sides together, pin the two nine-patch squares together, matching the seams. Use a ¼-inch (0.6-cm) seam and a stitch length of 12 (2.5 for metric machines); leave the presser-foot pressure slightly loosened. Sew clockwise around the perimeter, beginning in the middle of the upper edge of square 3 and ending in the middle of the upper edge of square 1. Turn the pillow right sides out, and stuff it with cut-up batting remnants. Sew the opening closed by hand.

The pillow is machine-washable on a warm and gentle cycle. Dry it alternately on warm and fluff settings.

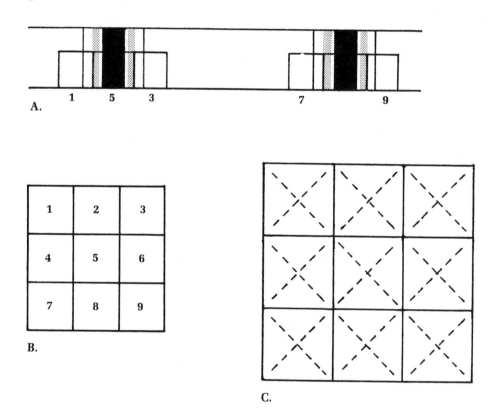

Figure 30.   "Woven-Look" Patchwork Pillow.
A. If a remnant is striped vertically, use squares 1 and 3 as patterns to cut squares 7 and 9; lay 1 and 3 over the repeat of the stripe pattern and align the stripes exactly.
B. Nine-patch with numbered squares to indicate assembly order.
C. The quilt stitching is done in diagonal lines across each square, with no quilting on the beginning or the ending inch.

Index